Catamaran Crossing

A Sailing Adventure

from

La Coruña to Antigua

Douglas Carl Fricke

Published by Allodium Chase
Copyright © 2025 by Douglas Carl Fricke. All Rights Reserved.

Except as permitted under the United States Copyright Act of 1976, no portion of the contents of this publication may be reproduced or transmitted in any form or by any means, electronic or mechanical, including photocopying, recording or by any information storage and retrieval system, without written permission of the author.

The story is based on a true adventure but for privacy reasons some character names have been disguised.

ISBN-13: 978-0-9799967-8-8

Dreams of sailing the ocean blue sometimes come true.

For Captain Ted and Joni

2021 Silver Medal Award

for Non-fiction in the Adventure Category

"Mr. Fricke has crafted a fascinating true-life tale that reads like a narrative work of fiction, and as such has all of the adventure, description, and immersive techniques that fiction writers use to pull us into the story."

K.C. Finn for Readers' Favorite

"An accomplished, knowledgeable sailor himself, Fricke's writing style is crisp, and the narrative is interesting and easy to follow."

Andrew at Jalbert Productions

"Informative and educational, it is only fitting that this is as good a quality of penmanship that you will see on the subject; and, the endorsement of John Shuttleworth is as good a reference as any."

Matt McAvoy, Senior Editor MJV Literary

 # Contents

Foreword by John Shuttleworth vii
Introduction ix
Opportunity Knocks 1
The Planning Stage 10
The Canary Islands 21
Detour to La Coruña, Spain 32
Decisions, Decisions 38
The Canary Current 49
Riding the Storm 61
Provisioning in the Canaries 77
The Real Club Náutico de Tenerife 93
Day 1: Say Good-bye to Santa Cruz 97
Day 2: Tropic of Cancer 105
Day 4: Migrant Swallow 108
Day 6: The Skipjack Tuna 112
Day 7: The Doldrums 116
Day 9: Flying Fish Contest 122
Day 10: Visitors 125
Day 12: Late-Night Flashback 131
Day 13: Sextant vs SatNav 136
Day 16: Land Ho! 145

Epilogue 156
About the Author 157
Acknowledgements 158

Map: The Canary Islands, (Wikimedia Commons)...................... 20
Map: Bay of Biscay, (Wikimedia Commons) 28
Artwork: *La naissance du catamaran* by Jean-Olivier Héro 31
Photo: Tower of Hércules 35
Schematic: Shuttleworth Design, *Spectrum-42*........................... 41
Photo: Main salon on starboard.. 44
Photo: *Toucan's* spinnaker, photo by Joni.................................... 54
Quote: Tristan Jones, *The Incredible Voyage*, 1977....................... 61
Photo: *Toucan's* winch farm, photo by Joni 83
Photo: First mate Joni in the galley... 90
Quote: H. G. Wells, *Time Machine*, 1895 104
Quote: Marcus Aurelius, *Meditations* 104
Artwork: The Flammarion Engraving.. 104
Quote: Jack London, *The Sea-Wolf*, 1904 108
Photo: Three sailors weighing the tuna, photo by Joni 115
Quote: Joseph Campbell, *Reflections on the Art of Living*............ 116
Quote: Hemingway, *The Old Man and the Sea*, 1952.................. 122
Illustration: Sextant (Wikimedia Commons) 136
Quote: Jules Verne, *Twenty Thousand Leagues Under the Seas* 136
Quote: Pythagoras, *The Symbols*, "Symbol 8" 145
Photo: The author on board *Toucan*, 1994, photo by Joni 157

 # Foreword by John Shuttleworth

I have been privileged to know many fine people who were or are still owners of my designs. A keen sailor myself, it was always important to me that my boats were used and loved by their owners. My passion for the sea and yacht design was expressed not just by the craft I was fortunate enough to create, but through the owners and their friends and families who enjoyed their vessels, and the fantastic experience of sailing a well-found yacht on the ocean.

When Ted invited me to sail with him and his crew from La Coruña to the Canaries in the summer of 1986, I leapt at the chance. I had met Doug, Ted and Joni and really got on well with them. We all seemed to share a zany sense of humour, and I knew we were in for a fun social time, as well as an adventure. The way the crew bonds together is particularly important if you are going to enjoy living in a small space for a week or so, and even more so if the going gets rough.

Doug's story of the voyage we did together, and the subsequent Atlantic crossing, makes fun reading. He adds in enough technical detail to explain some of the things that sailors need to know to safely attempt to go to sea in a small sailing yacht. Of course, the trip was more than having fun for me. Evaluating and experiencing my designs at sea and in difficult conditions has always been an integral part of my approach to design.

The last time I saw Ted, Joni, and Doug was when we met at Ted's house in Florida, where he has his stunning saltwater fish tanks, and watched the extremely funny video of the trip, ate a wonderful dinner together, and parted friends for life!

All the best,
John Shuttleworth

 # Introduction

It sounds like a simple plan:

- Take a three-week vacation in the summer.
- Fly to the Canary Islands and meet up with friends.
- Help sail their new catamaran across the Atlantic.

The vacation needs to be extended. Meeting up with friends turns out to be not so simple. And the last part of the plan…

Jump back to the 1980s, before the internet and cell phones, back when offshore cruising catamarans were coming of age and join us as we sail from La Coruña in northwest Spain to Antigua in the West Indies.

The islands, the cities, the yacht clubs, and the creatures are real, except for the mermaids. Mr. Shuttleworth, the man who designed the 42' catamaran *Toucan,* allowed the use of his real name, but the names of the other characters have been disguised for privacy reasons.

By convention, the names of the stars, planets, moons, meteor showers, and constellations have been capitalized. And following NASA's lead, the same is true for every reference to the Sun and the Moon.

May you find our adventure entertaining and informative.

The 42' Shuttleworth catamaran *Toucan* in the Bay of Biscay, May 1986

 **Opportunity Knocks**

April weather on Florida's Suncoast is some of the best for sailing. No more jackets against the wind chill and only a glimpse of the hot muggy days yet to come. It doesn't get any better than this.

The next regatta is three weeks away, so today I'm taking the boat out for a solo pleasure cruise. The anchor and chain are stashed in the locker. The mainsail is trimmed tight, and the large genoa sail is folded on deck ready to hoist. I motor-sail the trimaran into the Gulf of Mexico, shut off the engine, and raise the genoa sharply. Grabbing the helm again I turn the bow off the wind so the warm air flowing between the sails can lift the boat across the water.

This weekend sailor feels alive once again. With the tiller braced to steer a straight course, I climb down below to grab a bottle of water and my sunglasses. Back in the cockpit, I free the tiller and head up closer to the wind. It's times like this when my number one fantasy kicks in. Sell the house, the furniture, the rusty Ford, and quit my job. Broaden my horizons beyond the Suncoast and sail away to the Caribbean. But I can't quite make the break. My little world won't let me go.

***

Six days later, on a quiet Friday at the office, I slip out early and stop by the house. It's a two-bedroom place in an established neighborhood high on a ridge, a lofty fifty-four feet above sea level. I change into casual attire, then drive south on Highway 19.

The city of St. Petersburg on the Gulf Coast of Florida is situated on a peninsula separated from the mainland by Tampa Bay to the east. With so much water, the city has more than its share of bridges and a vibrant boating community. All along the waterfront, yacht clubs and sailing squadrons host well attended regattas. But for the competitors who must reposition their sailboats to and from the events, the numerous bridges always present a challenge.

As I drive across Pinellas Bayway on the south side of town, the wind funnels around the pillars of condo towers and ripples the surface of Boca Ciega Bay where a dozen small sailboats are racing, jockeying toward the favored end of the starting line. If the weather is like this tomorrow, I'm going sailing again.

Up ahead there's one more bridge to cross and I'll be on time for the dinner party. Whoa, what's this? Sirens blaring and yellow caution lights begin to flash. The cars in front of me slow to a stop. The gates come down across both lanes and the iron grate roadway of the bascule bridge rises over the Intracoastal Waterway.

Stuck in traffic, I turn the radio on hoping to hear a favorite tune. Instead, a news broadcaster blabbers about First Lady Nancy Reagan's new "Just Say No" drug awareness campaign. Another station replays some asinine commercial about a new and improved something or other. That's enough, I switch it back off.

Now we wait for one sailboat to pass. It doesn't seem fair that ten or more cars have to idle on both sides of the bridge, especially during the Friday afternoon rush hour. Unless, of course, you're on the boat.

Years ago, south of the Bayway and before the bridges, only Mother Nature lived on these mangrove barrier islands. Today the area is called Tierra Verde and new houses have been built only a few feet above sea level. My sailing friends Ted and Joni live out here. Their place is ideally situated on one of the canals so they can take their boat into the Gulf or Tampa Bay without being delayed at the drawbridges.

The lights stop flashing, the gates go up, and I follow the cars rushing into the neighborhood. The sirens seem to be following close behind. We're all breaking the speed limit but for some crazy reason a sneaky cop in an unmarked vehicle selects my ugly Ranchero and pulls me over.

Ford Rancheros are practical, two-door coupes with a backend cargo bay like pickup trucks. Mine was ugly on the day I bought it. The seller had it parked out front of a Texaco station with the hood open and a For Sale sign taped to the back window. The new paint job, dark green with bright pinstripes, turned me off and I still don't like it. But when I saw the pristine engine compartment and the polished chrome air cleaner on the carburetor, I couldn't pass it up. Some of the body parts are corroded now, but so what? It runs great, and the cargo bay is perfect for hauling sailing gear to and from the dock.

Maybe the officer standing at my window doesn't like the tacky pinstripes either.

"In a hurry?" he asks.

"Just goin' with the flow." I hand over my driver's license and vehicle registration card. Now I'm definitely late for dinner.

The man in uniform flips the shades up on his glasses and reads my name on the license.

"Is it pronounced Frick or Frickey?"

"It rhymes with tricky."

I think to myself, *Old friends call me Frick but call me whatever you want. Just hurry up.*

"Okay, Mr. Fricke. I'm giving you a warning today." He hands my IDs back. "Keep it under thirty-five on this side of the bridge."

What a streak of luck! There's a six-pack of brewski behind my seat and most other days an open bottle would be within easy reach.

***

On the front porch, Ted stands tall in the doorway. At six-three, he is about a head taller than me and could easily crush some bones with a firm handshake. He doesn't and probably never would.

"I'm a little late. Got stopped at the bridge and a cop pulled me over for speeding."

Ted glances at the old Ranchero. "Damn. I should have told you about the speed trap. They've been out there every day this week."

"It was only a warning ticket."

"Good. Come on in."

Once inside the double wooden doors and through the foyer, we enter a vaulted living space two stories tall. The ceiling slants toward the far wall of windows offering a view of their boat dock on the canal. Artwork acquired during a visit to the American Southwest graces the walls and shelves. Handwoven Navajo rugs and blankets are scattered about.

When Joni sees us, she shuts off the faucet and dries her hands. She's wearing a flowery T-shirt over baggy shorts as she greets me with her usual sisterly hug and takes the six-pack.

"There's still two cold ones in the fridge from last time."

"I'll trade you for one of 'em."

Fesser, their pet cockatiel, takes off and flies around the living room. While we watch his confined aerobatics, another bird screeches from its cage. It's a white, sulphur-crested cockatoo, probably jealous of Fesser, whose wings aren't clipped. Joni pulls the cover over Sugar's cage and the piercing cries stop.

"This bird could live another forty years." Her tone sounds like a complaint, but it's no secret Joni loves her pets. She's the outdoorsy type and will sometimes watch for hours to get the perfect zoomed-in photo of a feathered friend in Fort De Soto Park. In the heat of the day, she'll gather her chestnut brown hair under a wide-brim sun hat.

Ted says, "There's a cockatoo over fifty years old up north in a Chicago zoo."

Fesser lands on Joni's shoulder, lifts his head and whistles.

Ted picks up his drink and beckons us to follow him. His casual, short sleeve shirt, open at the collar, hangs loose over light grey slacks. And like most tropical sailors, he wears weathered deck shoes without socks.

We accompany him into the living room where he recently built a saltwater aquarium in one of the walls so that it can be viewed from two sides. The wiring and plumbing, cleverly hidden in the wall, go through the floorboards into his workshop on the lower level, which is stocked with every imaginable household tool.

The last time I was here, colorful tropical fish brought back from dive trips to the Florida Keys swam in the aquarium. This time the tank appears empty until something slithers up the glass. The creature blends perfectly with its surroundings, making it hard to identify, but then a row of light-colored suckers on the underside of a coiled tentacle gives it away.

"You've got an octopus!"

"Kinda hard to see, isn't he?" Joni brushes her fingers on the glass. "We named him Penner, our friendly little *octopus vulgaris*."

Ted slides the heavy top of the tank off to the side. "We found him out in the Gulf. Actually, he found us. Go ahead. Put your hand in."

Yeah, right. Each tentacle is about the same thickness as my forefinger but much longer. Joni offers no encouragement, no warning. She just smiles, and the cockatiel on her shoulder bobs his head back and forth.

"Maybe I will, after you show me how it's done."

"Okay, watch." Ted lowers his hand into the tank and the octopus curls one of its tentacles around a finger. The creature reaches for another, but as Ted slowly raises his hand out of the water, the octopus releases its grip.

"Put your hand in so you can feel its strength," says Ted. "And don't jerk it out because you could rip off some of its suckers."

Ted's a big man but wouldn't hurt a flea. I place my empty beer bottle on the shelf, lift my arm, and reach into the saltwater. The little octopus holds tight to the side of the tank with six or seven tentacles, wraps another one around my finger, and squeezes. Following Ted's lead, I pull my hand away slowly and overpower little Penner.

"He sure has a strong grip. Let's hope we never have to tangle with his big brother in the wild." An itchy sensation lingers in my finger as I wipe my hand on the seat of my pants and retrieve the beer bottle.

The aquarium and the whole setup is quite impressive. I point toward the tank. "It's clever the way you built it into the wall."

"Thanks." Ted slides the top on again and places a brick in the middle to secure it. "I'll show you the filtering system later."

Joni leads the way back to the kitchen past the windows facing the dock. A snowy egret stands steadfast on the seawall staring into the water, feathers reflecting pink from the red sky at sunset.

"Where's your sailboat?"

"We sold it." Ted swirls the ice cubes in his glass. "We're having a new one built in southern England."

"You're kidding me."

Joni refills her wine glass and freshens Ted's drink. She grabs the other bottle from the fridge and pops the cap off with the cast-iron opener screwed to the wall. Grinning, she takes my empty bottle and hands me the cold one. We join Ted at the counter separating the kitchen from the living room.

"Why did you decide to have the boat built in England?"

"We chose a design by John Shuttleworth, who lives on the Isle of Wight," says Ted. "He recommended a builder close by, so he could supervise the construction and check on the progress."

Several years ago, Shuttleworth gained international recognition in the sailing community when a trimaran he designed took first place in the TwoSTAR transatlantic race. He's well-known in the world of offshore multihulled sailboats and routinely publishes articles in *Multihulls Magazine*.

"Good move. I've read a number of his essays. He's ahead of the competition, no question about it."

Ted clears his throat. "It's a catamaran, a *Spectrum-42*."

Wow! Adding a Shuttleworth design to the club fleet will be exciting news for the members. Before I can say anything, Joni launches Fesser off her finger and turns toward me.

"During construction Ted and I can do some sightseeing in southern England and visit the boatyard all in one trip."

Ted finishes another sip of his drink. "The deciding factor was the favorable exchange rate." He cracks a smile. "The dollar is much stronger in Europe these days."

As Ted continues talking about the boat deal, I keep wondering what it would be like to sail from England to Florida. I have dreamed of sailing west from St. Pete straight across the Gulf to Corpus Christi, Texas or maybe south into the Caribbean, but not across the ocean. The biggest hurdle has been finding a compatible mix of experienced crew. Sailing with Ted and Joni on the Gulf Coast, in their boat or mine, has always been a delight—compatibility being the least of our concerns.

The Spectrum-42 is four feet longer than my trimaran and will easily accommodate five sailors. What would I say if they asked me to help with the delivery?

Fesser finalizes another flight around the room and lands on the back of an empty bar stool. Ted whistles a melody, and the bird repeats it almost exactly. Joni's amused. She's acting funny, and I don't know why.

The cockatiel easily makes the jump to Ted's shoulder and quick as a wink, an image flashes before my eyes—a pirate with a parrot. Turning on my stool, I glance at the bird, then at Ted. "How will the boat arrive here in St. Pete?"

"I planned to have it delivered but Joni keeps talking about sailing it across ourselves."

"That's right." Joni looks excited and profoundly serious. "We could sail it across if you'd go with us."

After enjoying another one of Joni's baked fish dinners with steamed veggies, we sit around the dining room table and talk for hours. Are we seriously thinking about sailing across the ocean in a forty-two foot boat?

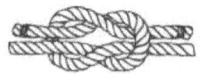 ## The Planning Stage

Crossing the Atlantic will be the longest sailing voyage any of us have ever taken, and preparations will require far more planning than we needed for our quick jaunts up and down the west coast of Florida.

No sailing today, I changed my mind. There's groundwork to do. It starts with a visit to the card catalog in the branch library on Fifth Avenue. Two of the books that sound promising are situated on the shelf in the right spot. The librarian says she can requisition the others from the main library and have them available for pick-up by Monday afternoon.

"By Monday? Thanks anyway. I'll drive downtown right now."

Back home, the books get stacked on the end table by the front door, all but the hardcover featuring the Canary Islands. Flipping through the pages reminds me to check my passport.

Here it is, in the center drawer of the roll-top desk. Most of the visa stamps are from short visits to island nations in the Caribbean. But there's this one page filled entirely with entry/exit dates and logograms posted by customs officials in Beijing during a summer-long business trip. Fortunately, the passport won't expire until late '87.

As the attic fan in the hallway pulls fresh air in through the jalousie windows, a rattling sound snaps me out of my daydreams. The back door is wide open, and a gray squirrel has wandered in looking for a handout. She's my only so-called pet and has been hanging around for years, easily recognizable by the v-shaped battle scar on her left ear. When I clap my hands, she scurries out onto the patio and waits for me to follow with a handful of peanuts. Two younger squirrels chase each other in circles up a tree trunk by the fence.

I can't stop thinking about sailing the Atlantic. What an amazing opportunity, especially with Ted and Joni on a new Shuttleworth catamaran. I'm spacing out, wondering about my family up north. Should I tell Dad or my sisters about this trip? No, Dad will worry too much. I'll tell them all about it when we get back.

The phone rings. I toss the rest of the nuts and answer it.

It's Jim Hoff.

We've been close friends since high school, so I guess that makes it okay to skip the part about 'Hello, how are you?'. He just starts right in.

"Hey Frick, what're you doin'?"

After we finished tours of Southeast Asia with the Army, we both returned to hometown Cincy for about four years then migrated south to St. Pete. Maybe it had something to do with the weather.

We shared an apartment for a year, one block off the beach, before Jim moved into town with his girlfriend. That's when I took out a loan for this bachelor pad.

Hoff doesn't wait for an answer. "We're throwing a birthday party tonight at Billy's place. He'll be forty, like you—old man."

"Yeah, sure." That probably didn't sound too enthusiastic.

He says, "What? Just show up."

"Last night, I kinda agreed to help some friends sail a new catamaran across the Atlantic."

"Far out! Who are they? Have I ever met them?"

"Don't think so. They're members of the sailing club. Last year the three of us sailed on my boat down to the Keys. Lots of fun."

"So, they're buying a boat to sail across the ocean and want to recruit you as crew. What is he—a doctor, a lawyer, a lottery winner?"

"He's a pathologist getting ready to retire. But, more importantly, he's a friend and an easygoing skipper. We call him Captain Ted."

"That's better than Dr. Ted."

"Oh, and get this. His first mate, who's closer to our age, loves to cook. You should see her kitchen."

"You're thinking about going, aren't you?" says Hoff.

"Damn straight but haven't actually committed yet."

"Whatta you mean? Why not?"

"I'll need to take three weeks off work without pay."

"No big deal, you've done that before."

He's right. However, "There's a race in Clearwater next month."

"You can miss one frickin' race."

"Plus, my boat will need to be hauled out of the water."

That means hiring a crane operator, rent for the boatyard at Bowlees Creek, and paying the crane guy again to lift the boat back in.

"Quit making excuses. When are you leaving?" Hoff wants to know.

"Well, if I go, it'll be a couple of weeks yet."

Damn, I'm gonna have to get my butt in gear. "Can you sail down to Sarasota Bay next weekend with me to get the boat hauled out?"

"Sure, come over to Billy's tonight, and we'll talk about it."

Hoff worked for a while with a tugboat operation in the Gulf and likes being out on the water. That's something else he and I have in common. We enjoy being team members in demanding situations, ready to deal with possible dangers. Could it be the army training drilled into us? If I could finance a sailing adventure like this one, Hoff would be invited for sure.

"Bring your own beer," he says and hangs up.

"All right, see you later."

He's already gone.

Back out on the patio, the fat belly squirrel has stopped eating the peanuts and is now burying them in the garden. That's all for today, you little fuzz butt.

***

After partying too hard at Billy's, I slept in late this morning. Still hungover after a shower and two tabs of Excedrin, I pick up the phone and call Joni just to touch base and double check to see if maybe they were joking—a slim possibility.

She answers before the second ring. We chitchat a bit then she says, "Come over Wednesday after work for dinner. We borrowed some more books from the library and Ted wants to have another brainstorming session."

"Okay. Tomorrow at work I'll talk to my supervisor about taking some time off. If he gives me any grief, I'm prepared to call it quits."

"Good luck. See you Wednesday."

At the office I spend most of my time installing updates to the operating systems, teaching, and helping rocket scientists debug their programs. The routine daily grind, the same old commute, and the short weekends have taken their toll. I need another vacation with some excitement, to feel alive again.

Two years ago the corporate giant sent me overseas for three months and co-workers covered for me. If they could handle that, they can surely handle a three-week absence.

***

Wednesday evening after dinner, the planning discussion continues. Ted has a stack of sailing magazines on the chair next to him. Articles about the trade winds, the ocean currents, the hurricane season, and the Caribbean Islands help us settle on the best time of year and the best route. It's a no-brainer. The only reasonable route follows the easterly trade winds which start near the Canary Islands and blow steadily across the mid-Atlantic toward the Caribbean all year long. They're safest in late spring before the hurricanes start forming.

Joni asks, "How'd it go with your supervisor?"

"We had lunch yesterday. He's also a sailor, not much older than me, and races a Hobie Cat with his teenage son on weekends."

Ted looks up from a sailing magazine. "Sounds good so far."

"When I broke the news, he actually shared my excitement and said he'll find a way to let me have the time off."

Fesser takes wing from the kitchen, flies two laps around the living room, and lands on top of his cage.

Ted closes the magazine. "Excellent, I've got some other good news. Last month when I told my co-workers at the hospital about our plans, an intern from Spain suggested we stop in the Canaries. He said his father's been a member of the yacht club on the island of Tenerife for years."

"Apparently he's also a bigwig at the club," adds Joni.

Ted whips out a *par avion* envelope bearing three postage stamps from Spain. "And yesterday in the mail, we received this special guest invitation from Don Fernando promising a warm welcome if we decide to visit the club."

"That's a great connection, like transatlantic reciprocity between yacht clubs."

Joni smiles as she takes a sip of wine. "Are you gonna go with us?"

"Yes, absolutely."

Did I just feel my heartbeat stutter?

"So glad you can join us." Ted flashes a big smile my way.

That settles it then. I'm committed. Now we have a team of three sailors and the plans are taking shape. On my way out the door, I say, "I'll check for other books on navigation at the library and at Haslam's Book Store."

Joni's keyed up too. "And I'll stop at Barnes & Noble to browse through their travel books."

***

Before they depart for England to take delivery of their new boat, Ted and Joni divide the sailing trip into three stages. The plan sounds simple enough. Once the catamaran is launched, they'll sail to the Canary Islands with two of the boat builders as crew and I'll rendezvous with them at the yacht club on Tenerife. We'll cross the Atlantic to the Caribbean in the second stage, and in the final stage, sail north to Florida.

By then, well over five thousand nautical miles will be recorded in the logbook.

I stuck around St. Petersburg for two weeks getting ready for the trip. Now it's Friday afternoon, and I'm sitting at my desk tweaking software modules but mostly daydreaming and getting antsy. Sure hope there's no delay with the launch. The boatyard, where the catamaran is being built, is located near the English Channel in the town of Topsham on the River Exe. It's five hours later there so maybe they'll call me tomorrow at home. Nope, the phone rings.

"Hello, it's Ted. Can you hear me okay?"

"Yeah, you just sound far away."

He's probably standing in one of those red telephone boxes, a true British cultural icon, with Joni at his side ready to hand him another fistful of coins in case the long-distance operator wants more.

Ted says, "I'm calling from the boatyard with good news. The boat was launched this week, and after the final sea trial and a shakedown tomorrow, we'll set sail Monday morning."

The trip to the Canaries will take at least seven days.

"That's super! I'll make flight arrangements to arrive on Tenerife the following Monday."

"We may be there by then," says Ted. "Oh, there's one other thing. We decided to name the catamaran *Toucan*."

"Cool, another bird in the family. See you next week."

***

An uncluttered life as a single man makes it easy to prepare for the trip. My sailboat, a racing trimaran, rests high and dry in the boatyard, and good buddy Jim agrees to check on the house and pick up the mail. With the home front taken care of, I hand-deliver the expected vacation notice to my supervisor. He wishes me good luck. I feel like I've been set free, footloose.

Now, with a confirmed departure date, I swing by the travel agency on Central to book a flight and request a long layover in Madrid. The agent asks about a return flight, so I tell her about the sailing plans. She says, "Oh dear! Be careful out there."

A few days later I'm up before sunrise and mill around the house. Double-check the flight tickets and traveler's checks, pack my bags, clean out the fridge, and squeeze the Ranchero into the garage. Hoff shows up with his El Camino and we drive up 49th Street to Biff Burger. It's a typical open-air kind of place, no doors.

Kenny sees us, vacates his barstool, and joins us at a picnic table farthest from the street. He and Hoff spend way too many weekends on the golf course. Here in Florida that's year round.

He slides in next to me. "What're you two up to?"

"Takin' Fricke to the airport," says Hoff. "He's gonna sail across the Atlantic."

"No shit?" Kenny glances my way. "You're crazier than I thought."

"You would know." I smile and give him a brief description of the sailing plans. He shakes his head and changes the subject to his latest strategy for improving his golf game. Says he needs to keep his left arm straight and his head down during the swing.

Hoff and I finish our burgers while Kenny rambles on about his putting game. The waitress sees that I'm raring to go and drops the check on the table. I pick it up and start for the checkout counter.

"Hey Kenny, I'll let you buy me a beer when I get back."

Hoff has the El Camino fired up already.

Midday traffic is light on the bridge as we drive across the bay to Tampa International. The windows are rolled down, and there's no need for small talk; never is with Hoff.

Two brown pelicans gliding close to the guardrail stay aloft with the wind gusts from the rush of oncoming traffic.

When we arrive at the airport terminal, I get the impression that Hoff is running late. He stays in the driver's seat and reaches for my hand through the passenger side window.

"Okay, sailor man, take care out there," he says. "And send me a postcard from Atlantis."

"Ha! Will do." I slip him a five-spot for gas. "Thanks for the lift. See you next month."

***

The Pan Am jumbo jet is less than half full as it backs away from the gate. These transatlantic flights to Europe take all night, so I might be able to catch some shut-eye. After the stewardess serves dinner and dims the cabin lights, I move to a section with empty rows and recline all the way back without disturbing anyone.

Touching down at Madrid-Barajas Airport jars me awake. We disembark and merge into the bustling main terminal. Surprisingly, there's no line at the currency exchange kiosk. The cashier converts my

C-notes and smaller bills into pesetas, though the exchange rate isn't quite what I expected. I should have swapped my dollars at a local bank in the States. Oh well—live and learn.

Now, let's see if I can pull off a day-tripper plan during this six-hour layover. My luggage will be secure and transferred to the connecting flight, so rather than hang around the terminal, I take a bus into the city with one destination in mind: not the bullring, but the magnificent *Museo del Prado*. Hey, if I'm late getting back, I'll find a hotel for tonight and catch up with my bag tomorrow.

None of my friends would ever think of me as a museum enthusiast—I'm not. I simply want to see the place and do a quick walk-through, no specific artwork in mind. A self-guided tour brings back memories of elementary school days running with busloads of classmates through the Art Museum in Cincinnati's Eden Park, paying little or no attention to the exhibits. Here, it's vastly different. Large, well-preserved oil paintings—centuries old, by world-renowned European artists—capture my imagination at every turn.

On the bus back to the airport, I vow to return someday to Madrid's famous museum for more than just a couple of hours. The big board in the terminal displays the gate number for my flight, and with time to spare, I stop at a tapas bar for a slice of tortilla paisana before boarding the southbound plane to Santa Cruz de Tenerife in the Canary Islands.

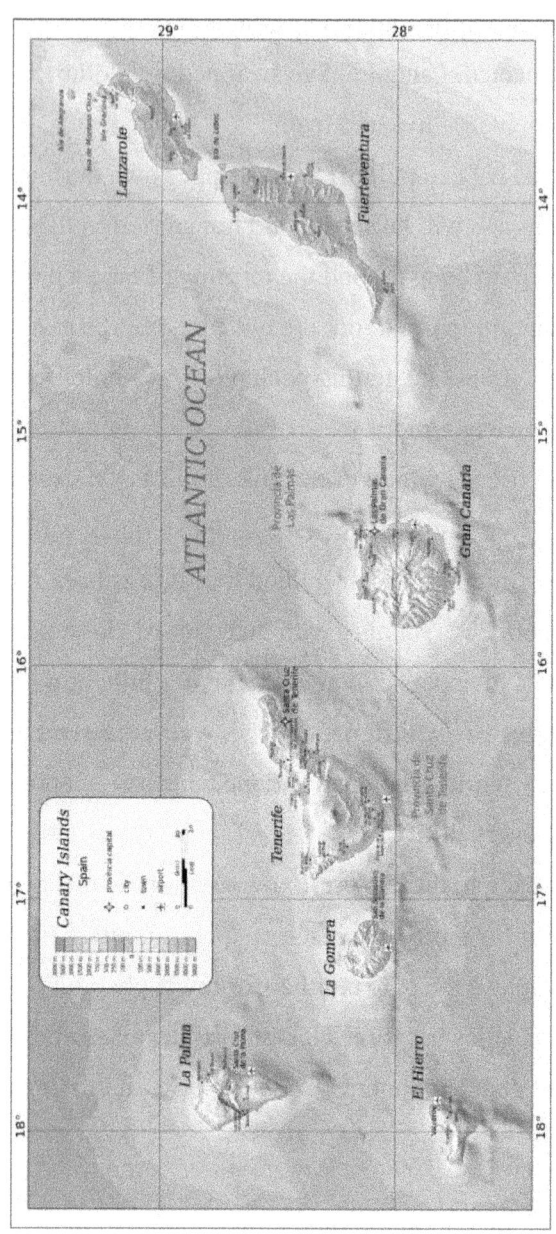

The Canary Islands, Spain

 # The Canary Islands

The customs inspector at Reina Sofía Airport waves me through without opening my bags. Whew! I'm never really sure about what might be verboten. Moving right along, I follow the signs and symbols to the rental car agencies. A bilingual agent completes the paperwork, hands over a set of keys, and unfolds a map of the island on the countertop.

Tenerife, the largest and most populous of the seven Canary Islands, has long been a vacation spot for the European tourist crowds. The Spanish archipelago lies in the subtropical zone less than a hundred miles off the coast of Morocco and offers year-round springlike weather with spectacular beaches and a bit of everything else—lush forests, exotic fauna and flora, deserts, mountains, and the active volcano Mount Teide.

Picturesque Santa Cruz is the capital city. Most of the residents, numbering not quite two hundred thousand, are of European origin primarily from Spain and Portugal. Also mixed in are descendants of the island's original inhabitants, the Guanches. For us sailors, this coastal city will serve as a maintenance and provisioning port before the long haul across the mid-Atlantic.

"What's your destination, *señor?*"

"The yacht club."

The agent highlights the location on the map. "It's on the northeast side of town, the Real Club Náutico on Avenida de Anaga."

When I thank her, she points toward the exit to the parking lot.

Traveling solo has its benefits. I can sleep or eat anytime, anywhere, without having to compromise with a companion. But this afternoon, I'd rather meet up with Ted and Joni. So, before finding a hotel or getting a bite to eat, I drive the Peugeot sedan through the city center to the yacht club.

From the sidewalk, I scan the private marina from behind a chainlink fence only half expecting to see the Shuttleworth boat tied to a dock. Traditional monohull sailboats and motor yachts occupy all the boat slips. No wide catamarans.

Last night on the plane, I didn't get much sleep. It's been a long day, and I know I'm being overly optimistic. Still, I want to check one more place before it gets dark, then search for a hotel.

After a short drive north along the island's rugged shoreline, I park at a cliffside vantage point and stand at the guardrail. The wind carries a trace of desert heat from the Sahara. I scan the horizon hoping to spot *Toucan*. With two hulls and an upright mast, a catamaran should be easy to spot from up here. But only a ferry packed with tourists from Gran Canaria plows through the waves. Not a single sailboat in sight. They'll show up tomorrow.

The Sun dips behind the mountain as the road curves back toward town. I turn into a hillside neighborhood near the yacht club. Tall cactus plants in a rock garden are in bloom with reddish-green flowers. Ahead, on a narrow street, a small hotel glows quietly in the dusk. The neon sign in the window reads "*habitación libre*"—a vacancy. It looks intriguing. Now I need to find a place to park. Circling the block, several restaurants are still open, but the stores are all closed. A spot opens up on the second round when a delivery van pulls away.

The hotel lobby, decorated with healthy potted plants, resembles a family living room in a guest house. The elderly clerk at the reception desk greets me with a friendly nod but when he hears my accented "*Hola,*" he beckons a young lady from the back room, probably his daughter. She understands my request and agrees to offer the room on a day-to-day basis. With a pleasant smile, she introduces herself as Maria and seems to enjoy practicing her English with me. We chat for quite a while about the tourist attractions, nearby beaches, and the best places to eat.

Another guest arrives at the reception desk, so I back away and pick up my bag. Maria looks annoyed by the interruption and adds a final suggestion, "You should visit my uncle's bodega down the street."

"Bodega?"

"Oh, sorry," she says, "the vintry, the neighborhood winery."

***

At the crack of dawn, fresh from a good night's sleep, I roll out of bed, get dressed, and go for a walk around the neighborhood. The high humidity combined with the salty ocean breeze makes the place feel like St. Pete. Seagulls squawk and chase each other in flight. A coffee shop on the corner and a bakery next door are preparing to open. I stroll past the rental car to make sure it wasn't towed away during the night and continue down the street to find the bodega.

Sheltering my eyes from the morning light with both hands, I gaze in the front window. It's a cozy little winery and I'm sure Ted and Joni will enjoy it—if they ever show up. Or maybe I should invite Maria to join me for a glass of wine. Is that the hint she dropped? No, she's friendly with all the guests. What am I thinking?

For the better part of the day, I drive around town taking in the sights, searching for other places of interest. Ted may need something from a hardware store and Joni will want to shop at the city's largest food market. Mid-afternoon I stop at the marina again but still see no sign of *Toucan*, then head back to the hotel.

"Hello, Mr. Fricke. How do you like Santa Cruz?" asks Maria as she slides my room key across the countertop.

"It's a beautiful city. Oh, I found the bodega this morning and peeked in the window." Wait, she probably doesn't know that word.

She frowns. "What did you say about the window?"

I had to laugh. "Peeked is like looked." Holding my hands on either side of my face. "I peeked in the window."

With a smile full of mischief, she moves out from behind the counter and beckons for me to follow her to the other side of the lobby. She's wearing a halter top and a flowery skirt that doesn't reach anywhere near her knees. She's probably young enough to be my daughter.

She almost whispers. "My papa don't want me to talk to the guests, but I need to learn better English."

"I'd be happy to help."

Have I invited trouble?

"Later today I work at the bodega." She glances back toward the front desk. "We could meet about 5 p.m."

She shows up right on time and it doesn't take long to realize that Maria is an excellent student genuinely interested in improving her command of the English language. She has a list of words to practice and a homework assignment to review. She's empowered, a quick learner. What a pleasure it is to teach an enthusiastic student.

***

At the front desk in the morning, Maria thanks me again for helping with her lessons and includes a few new words from her expanding vocabulary while we chat. Sure wish it was the other way around, that she was teaching me Spanish.

The drive into town from the hotel follows a creek down to the waterfront. I park close to the ferry terminal and wander out onto the wharf to find a well-placed bench with a view of the waterway approaching the yacht club's marina. Pelicans and seagulls are paying close attention to a young boy as he tosses his net into a school of bait fish shimmering close to the pilings. The birds aren't getting a free lunch yet.

What if Ted and Joni arrive in the middle of the night? Somebody at the Club Náutico needs to know how to contact me at the hotel.

***

It's always a good idea to read about the local culture before visiting a foreign country for the first time. Learn about the history and practice a few basic phrases. I'd never open a conversation with the inconsiderate greeting "Do you speak English?" Merchants may tolerate it because they want to sell their products, but most other people appreciate it when a foreigner at least knows how to say "Hello, thank you, and good-bye." They'll know from your accent that you're not a local.

On the morning of the third day, I drive by the club to check-in with the dockmaster but arrive too early. A cup of coffee and an hour later, there's a doorman standing out front under a blue awning.

With the Peugeot parked at the curb, I walk up wearing baggy shorts, sandals, and a loose-fitting T-shirt embellished with a sailmaker's logo from last year's race.

Out of respect, I greet the man with, "*Buenos días.*"

The doorman hears the phrase pronounced incorrectly and probably labels me as a *turista* from England or the States. He peers down his nose at the sandals and stands there, hands clasped behind his back. The man's attitude and blue blazer with the club emblem sewn on his breast pocket present a bit of a challenge rather than a welcome.

This is just great. He's giving me the silent treatment. Maybe I should have worn socks with my sandals. I take a step closer and say slowly, "I'd like to speak with the dockmaster."

In Europe, most educated people speak some English, but *Señor* Doorman is not one of them, or he flat-out refuses. The man doesn't say "No," but his body language sure shows it. He moves directly in front of the door, refuses to even pretend like he understands, and enforces the club rules—members only, no *turistas* allowed.

The two of us stand under the awning while I ramble on in polite, simple English. I argue that it would be perfectly okay if I step inside for a few minutes to explain my mission to somebody in the front office. It doesn't work. The man is just doing his job.

During my travels, I often find it frustrating not being able to converse with the locals in their native tongue and this happens to be one of those times. Shaking my head, I walk back to the rental car.

***

It's early in the morning, my fourth day on the island, getting ready to head out. The communication problem with the yacht club has been bothering me all through the night. There's an easy solution. Maria at the reception desk could call the dockmaster for me. When I drop off the room key, she agrees, and I listen to her explanation of my predicament in Spanish. She hangs up, smiles, and says, "¡*No hay problema!*" She's so helpful, I'd like to give her a big hug.

After grabbing a cup of coffee and a couple pastries at the bakery next-door, I drive up the mountain road to the cliffside vantage point to scan the seascape once again for *Toucan*. No luck.

Where the hell are they?

At sunset when I stop back at the club, tight-lipped *Señor* Doorman gives me a sealed envelope. Sure wasn't expecting that. I tip my cap, say *"Muchas gracias"* with my touristy accent, and walk back to the car to open the envelope in private. The note is brief like a telegram.

"Will call your hotel tonight at 9 p.m." Signed, Captain Ted.

Finally, contact. Ted must have called the club, and somebody gave him the number of the hotel. Then it dawns on me. *Toucan* went ashore. To make the phone call, they had to sail into port somewhere. An unscheduled stop means trouble.

Back in the hotel room after a quick bite to eat, Maria calls and asks if I'll accept the charges for the overseas call.

"Yes, of course."

The air conditioner mounted in the window rumbles like a diesel truck idling in the alleyway. I should have shut it off.

Captain Ted speaks quickly. "I'm calling from a marina in northwest Spain. We sailed into a hellacious storm in the Bay of Biscay, lost a rudder, and took shelter at the seaport in La Coruña."

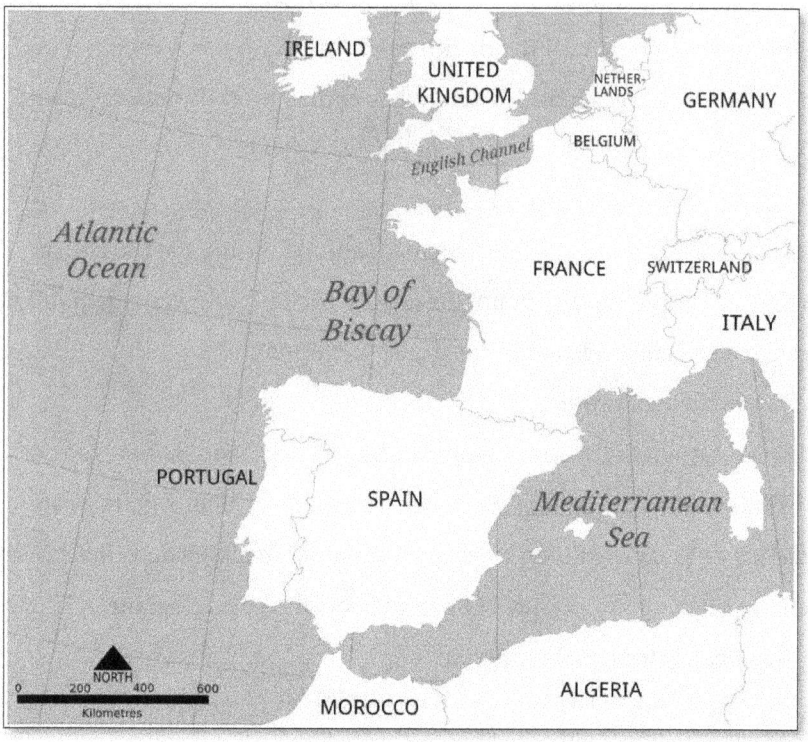

The Bay of Biscay, or Golfo de Vizcaya, is well-known to sailors as home to some of the North Atlantic's fiercest weather.

"Oh, shit! Was anybody hurt?" A sinking feeling churns in my gut. Someone may have been injured or swept overboard.

"No," says Ted. "Thank goodness."

What a relief!

"How bad is the boat damaged?"

"We'll fill you in when you get here. I have to make this call short."

Ted sounds on edge. Normally, he has a calm temperament.

I'm fidgeting with the phone cord. "I'll try to get a flight first thing in the morning."

"That'd be great," says Ted. "We'll be here for a couple more days and could use your help. Meet us tomorrow in La Coruña at the yacht club."

He ends the call, and I lower the handset to its cradle. Palm trees sway outside the window, but I might just as well be staring into empty space. The conversation ended too soon. The plans have changed, and lots of questions pop into my head. How in the hell did they lose a rudder? Did they sail through a patch of flotsam? I'd like to call right back but don't have the number.

Undressed, I slip under the bed sheet, my mind abuzz with thoughts of Ted and Joni.

We met by chance on Egmont Key, a secluded island state park at the mouth of Tampa Bay. Now, five years later, that sunny afternoon still seems so recent.

I had sailed in shortly before noon and dropped anchor in shallow water off the bayside beach about a hundred yards from another sailboat, a trimaran. It seemed like we had the whole island to ourselves. After settling in, I saw a woman on the shore and a man in the water next to his boat. Always curious and never shy, I thought I'd swing by to say hello.

Joni didn't notice my approach and continued to comb the beach for sand dollars while sidestepping horseshoe crab carcasses. Ted stood waist-deep scraping barnacles off the bottom of his boat; its name — *Sunburst*— painted on the side. When he spotted me, he came up onto the beach with a friendly smile. He had probably guessed what I wanted—to talk about boats.

He appeared to be in good physical condition, tall, and older than me because his hair had started to gray. His deep suntan certainly held stories of outdoor adventures, and I wanted to hear them someday.

Before I could speak, Joni shrieked. "Ted, look at your shorts!"

Dozens of crabby little barnacles clung to his swim trunks, so he waded into the water and brushed most of them off. Back on the beach, Joni spun him around and found a few more crawling in his hair and one in his ear. She flicked them away, which Ted and I found amusing.

Still chuckling, I said, "The little buggers really liked your shorts."

"Good thing they don't bite," replied Ted.

We fell into an easy conversation about our boats, and I told them about the new sailing club that was forming in the Tampa Bay area for catamaran and trimaran owners. In the years following, our friendship grew and so did the size of our sailboats. To this day we have a love of the sport in common and that keeps bringing us together.

***

I roll over and kick off the sheet. The noisy air conditioner is keeping me awake, not cool. Get up, switch it off, and fall back in bed. Shadows of palm fronds dance on the wall as I wonder what tomorrow will bring.

La naissance du catamaran by Jean-Olivier Héro

 ## Detour to La Coruña, Spain

Early the next morning at the reception desk, Maria sets my mind at ease when she says the flights to the mainland leave every day before noon. She slides an invoice across the counter with the charges for last night's collect call added at the bottom and watches as I sign over some traveler's checks.

She says, "When you return to Santa Cruz, stop by to say hello."

"If the plane is fully booked, I'll be back this afternoon." I pick up my bag and head for the door.

At the airport, the ticket agent for Iberia Airlines attaches a green ID tag on my luggage and drops it on the conveyor belt. "We'll be boarding at gate number three."

Shortly after take-off, Mount Teide drifts past my oval window and out of sight. According to one of the travel brochures, the volcano rises higher than any other peak in the Atlantic, over twelve thousand feet.

Often during the three-hour flight, I gaze out at the ocean below. Still thinking about the extent of *Toucan's* damage, I imagine one scenario after the next. Ted said they lost a rudder but didn't elaborate. Did the boat spring a leak? Is the steering mechanism bent out of shape? What about a replacement rudder? A major repair job will increase the overall costs and cause the trip to be delayed. If it takes weeks, I'll indeed lose my job.

The Iberian Coast comes into view as the plane begins its descent. If we were flying over the Gulf Coast of Florida, I could easily identify our location. However, now, I can't tell if we're north of Portugal yet. Not that it matters, but I may soon be sailing somewhere down there. Or maybe I'll be flying home to my desk job.

The stewardess delivers an announcement in Spanish, but I don't need a translation because the passengers across the aisle start adjusting their seat backs and tray tables to the upright and locked positions. She then walks down the aisle checking both sides to ensure that all seat belts are securely fastened. Her blue pillbox hat matches her uniform.

"Pardon me." I catch her attention. "How far is it to the city center?"

With an enjoyable accent, she says, "It's twelve kilometers, you can take a bus from the terminal."

Out front it's a bit nippy. But sure enough, a bus with its engine running and a driver behind the wheel displays its next destination above the windshield: La Coruña. The door is open, so I step aboard and greet the driver. He can tell I'm a tourist and selects the exact change for the fare from my handful of *pesetas*.

When the bus arrives at the main station, the driver kills the engine and opens the door. It's the end of the line. Stepping off, I see taxicabs parked along the sidewalk and three men poised next to the lead cab surveying the passengers as we disembark.

I approach them with my bag in hand and say, "Yacht club," loud enough for all to hear. Getting no response, I say it again. The cabbie with a ball cap speaks up, "Club Náutico?" He sees my wrinkled brow and repeats it. When I hear the local pronunciation of "club" a second time, the light bulb over my head comes on. He makes a welcome gesture toward the taxi at the front of the queue.

The man keeps quiet as he zigzags through the city; black rosary beads swinging from the rear-view mirror. We soon arrive at the only yacht club in town. The burgee flying on the flagstaff and the sign at the entrance to the driveway identify the building as the Real Club Náutico.

Holding up an index finger, I say, "*Un minuto.*" I get out without paying and walk over to the seawall expecting to catch a quick glimpse of *Toucan*. Not so easy. Hundreds of sailboats line the docks and others have anchored out in the harbor. This may take a while.

My tolerant driver is leaning against the front fender, smoking a hand-rolled cigarette. We settle the cab fare, and I wander farther down the seawall to continue the search.

A long rock jetty with a blinking navigational light at the end extends halfway across the inlet and protects the harbor from the sea. Off in the distance to the north, the massive lighthouse called the Tower of Hércules stands guard on high ground. I read about it on the plane. The ancient Roman structure, 180 feet tall, has been in constant use since the second century. That's well over a thousand years before Columbus sailed off the charts.

As I take in the harbor scene, the extreme low tide catches me by surprise. In Florida it only varies a few feet but up here in northern latitudes the difference between the highs and lows can vary as much as twenty. Right now, the tide is so low that some of the smaller boats rest on the muddy bottom close to the base of the steep seawall, stranded for hours until the tide comes back in. Fortunately for the boaters, the high and low times are quite predictable and published in tide tables by local newspapers.

Tower of Hércules, the ancient Roman lighthouse near La Coruña, Spain.

Killing time, I marvel at how the floating docks can ride up and down on tall pilings embedded in the bottom of the harbor. Ramps, hinged at the seawall, extend out to the docks to provide walkways. Each one has two little metal wheels at the end that allow the ramp to roll back and forth along the dock with the rise and fall of the tide—a clever solution.

The late afternoon Sun casts a warm glow as the shadows of umpteen masts stretch out across the marina. Just as I was about ready to give up the search and find the dockmaster to inquire about *Toucan*, a familiar voice sounds like music to my ears. "Hey, Frick!"

It's Joni with Ted and an older, gray-haired man. They're carrying bags of groceries. Ted smiles and shakes my hand. "Good to see you again!" He rests his hand on my shoulder for a few seconds.

Joni places a bag on the seawall and gives me a hug. She backs away and introduces her Uncle Jim from South London. His courteous handshake feels weak, accompanied by a quick nervous glance.

I greet him with a smile. "Nice to meet you."

When Joni says he'll be joining us, I can't help but wonder if he has any sailing experience. Even if he does, he's a senior citizen and probably sees himself as a passenger—just along for the ride. That might be all right for an afternoon sail, but this is a week-long, offshore voyage, and we could encounter some rough seas.

Ted breaks the silence. "Come on, let's get these groceries down to the boat."

I lift the bag Joni had been carrying and follow the party down the ramp past the little metal wheels and onto the crowded dock.

She turns her head and asks, "How was your flight?"

"It was a commuter plane, only half full."

I'm more interested to hear about *Toucan*. "How's the boat?"

"It's a beauty. You'll see it in a minute."

I quicken my pace to walk beside her.

Monohull sailboats in slips on either side of the dock outnumber the motor yachts. Then I see the catamaran for the first time, tied to one of the T-docks far from the seawall.

The sleek offshore cruiser is even more impressive than I imagined. It's wide and long but doesn't look heavy. This modern vessel with a shiny new paint job, tugging at its dock lines, seems to float on the surface like a water strider.

While I have my full attention on the boat, Joni takes the grocery bag from my arms and lifts it high to place it on the stern deck. I walk along the dock the length of the catamaran to admire its beauty.

Hello, *Toucan*. We could sail around the world with you.

But today, the damage from the storm is foremost in my thoughts. I know better than to fall in love at first sight. I've seen boats that look good but can't sail worth a crap. Before I can fall in love, I need to take her sailing, to feel how she responds to the wind and the waves.

An image pops into my head of a fancy sports car sitting at the curb with a front wheel missing and I can't help but wonder how long *Toucan's* repairs will take. We need to get the boat seaworthy again.

Joni must have read my mind. "John Shuttleworth is here. He flew in yesterday."

"He wants to inspect the boat before we go back out," says Ted.

"Great! Where is he?"

"Running errands," says Joni. "He'll be back shortly."

Ted brings me up to date. "I called him two days ago as soon as we noticed the missing rudder. He said he wanted to see the extent of the damage firsthand."

 **Decisions, Decisions**

Two of the young craftsmen who assisted with the boat construction also volunteered as crew to help sail *Toucan* on its maiden voyage. Losing one of the rudders during the fierce storm in the Bay of Biscay freaked them out so much that soon after taking shelter in La Coruña, they made excuses as to why they wouldn't continue the journey. Not surprisingly, none of their excuses had anything to do with the storm.

Ted and Joni have sailed with me for short trips to the Florida Keys and we feel confident about sailing the new boat, just the three of us. But for the offshore trip to Tenerife and for crossing the Atlantic, Ted wants at least one other crew member. I agree. We'd be able to divvy up the workload and there's room on the boat for another person. But finding a qualified sailor who is also easy-going will be difficult. With hesitancy, Joni drafted an enticing notice and posted it on the club's bulletin board.

Crew Wanted:

One experienced sailor to crew aboard a catamaran to the Canary Islands. Return airfare included. Inquire at the dockmaster's office.

Uncle Jim isn't a sailor. He simply accepted an invitation to go cruising with his niece and her husband. When Joni tells him about his cabin on starboard, he frowns. She points in the proper direction and says, "Starboard is on the right side, facing forward."

Uncle Jim asks, "Where'd *that* word come from?"

"It comes from Old English *steorbord*, literally 'side on which a vessel was steered'," Ted explains. "Ancient boat builders fastened the steering oar or paddle on the right side of the vessel."

"Probably because more people are right-handed," says Joni.

"Exactly," says Ted. "The captain would dock with the other side against the wharf, and it became known as the port side."

Uncle Jim lifts his eyebrows and nods, "Right, that makes sense."

"But with modern vessels, the steering device, called a rudder, is attached at or near the stern. With catamarans, each hull has a rudder." Ted shakes his head. "But not today with *Toucan*."

He fetches the telescoping aluminum pole, which serves as a boat hook, and guides the group toward the stern. Extending the pole, he passes it through the murky water under the hull to show how the rudder is missing, all of it.

"Any damage to the hull?" I ask.

"Not that I can see. Something hit the rudder during the storm and caused the shaft to shear off."

Joni says, "It could have been anything—a sea turtle, driftwood… who knows?"

Ted slides the boat hook back into the cockpit. "The hull's not leaking. That's the good news."

"Where were you when it happened?"

"Not sure, can't give you the exact location but it definitely happened during the storm." Ted scratches his head. "We didn't notice it missing until after we tied up to the dock."

What? Nobody noticed when the rudder disappeared? It must have been one hell of a storm. The wind howling and the waves roaring so loud nobody heard the crash. I wonder what else may be damaged.

"Did Shuttleworth say where we can get a replacement?"

"No. He said a new one will have to be fabricated. He's been making phone calls."

Ted doesn't look too pleased, staring off in the distance, pinching his chin. This doesn't sound good to me. We're now dependent on finding local services and none of us speaks Spanish.

While we're still on the dock next to the boat, Joni steps closer to me and explains the sleeping arrangements.

"Uncle Jim is on starboard, and Ted and I have the v-berth on port."

The catamaran, a combination of cruising comfort and racing performance, has v-shaped berths roomy enough for two passengers in the bow of each hull. Uncle Jim climbs aboard with caution and Joni hands him a bag of groceries.

Ted moves closer to me and says, "The aft cabin on our side has a single bunk and it's reserved for you."

Our eyes meet for an instant, in agreement. We both know that Joni would prefer to have another crew member, possibly a total stranger, on the other side of the boat.

I'm anxious to climb aboard but it's proper etiquette with a newly launched yacht to wait for an invitation. Joni offers one with a wave of her hand. "Come on."

Shuttleworth Design, Spectrum-42

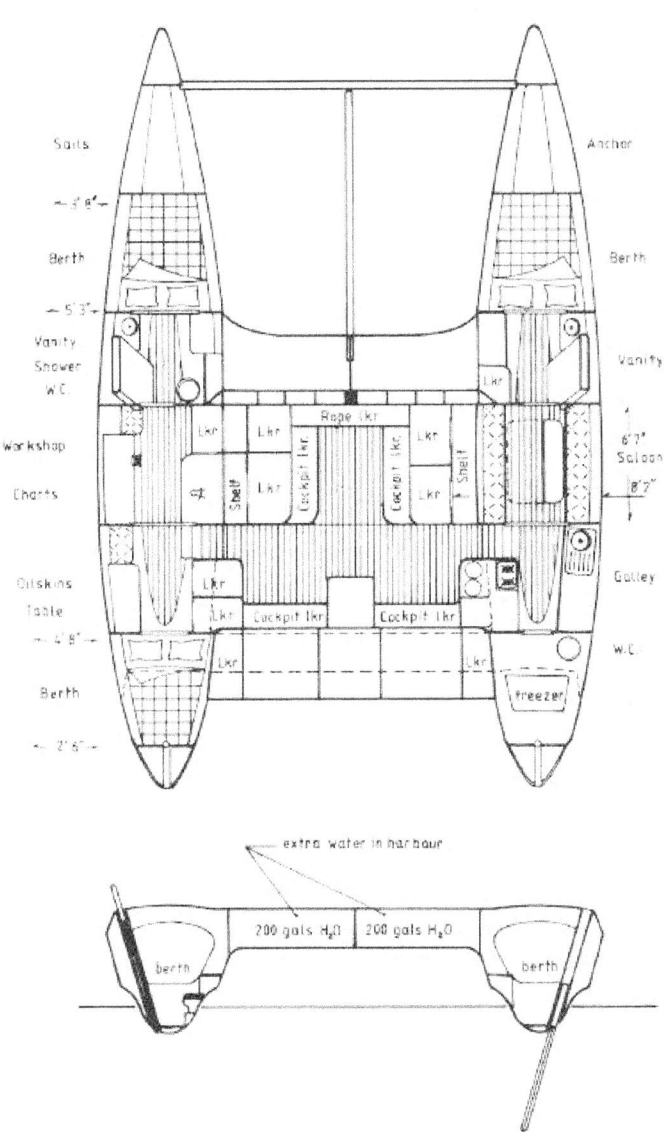

When I step aboard, the deck feels strong and well-built. The bench along the rear of the cockpit must measure fifteen feet between the two hulls. It's actually a long storage locker with four lids. I take a seat in the middle and rest my hand on top of the ship's wheel like a helmsman.

Toucan's stainless-steel wheel is about four feet in diameter and connected to a pedestal. On top of the pedestal, a large compass displays all its markings and numbers in glowing red under a dome. Next to the compass, a multifunction electronic device shows the boat's speed and the depth of the water.

Directly in front of the pedestal, a four-stroke, water-cooled diesel engine fits tightly within a compartment accessible through a trapdoor in the cockpit floor. Its drive shaft is linked to a propeller housing that is lowered into the water when needed.

The open bridgedeck design gives me an unobstructed view of the entire deck with easy access to all the winches. I can see the wind indicator atop the tall mast, a fractional rig, which stands in the center of a massive crossbeam connecting the two hulls. To achieve ultimate stiffness in the main crossbeam, the builders embedded carbon fibers across the full width of the boat and down into each hull, fanning out into reinforced areas. The remaining fibers in the crossbeam were laid in carefully determined directions to resist twisting and bending.

Joni hollers at me from the galley on starboard. "Grab your bag and go check out your cabin."

I enter the port side hull through the companionway by descending three steps down into the open center cabin. Turning and looking forward, the closed door that leads into the captain's quarters is maybe seven or eight feet away. The chart table and nav station are on my right. A workspace on the left consists of a narrow shelf with storage compartments below for tools and spare parts, brand new, some in unopened boxes.

All the interior components, like shelves, walls, doors, steps, *etc.*, were fabricated from lightweight panels, as in modern passenger airliners.

The aft cabin isn't a true cabin because there's no door for privacy. Sitting on the edge of the bunk, I can see out through the companionway when its sliding top is open. I lean all the way back. The on-off switch for the reading lamp, mounted in the ceiling, is within easy reach. The two shelves in the back corners are big enough to hold my cassette player, tapes, headphones, and paperbacks. And here's my favorite. The view through the escape hatch skims just above the waterline and below the rear crossbeam. This cozy space will be my sleeping quarters for the next four weeks. It's spartan perfect.

***

Ted is talking with someone in the cockpit. It's a man with a British accent but it doesn't sound like Uncle Jim. It must be John Shuttleworth. When I climb up, Ted lifts his right arm slightly in my direction and introduces me to the boat designer.

His genuine smile gives me a warm feeling, and I take a liking to him right away. He wears spectacles with round lenses like the ones Lennon made popular. A full beard and mustache match his reddish-brown hair. We're both of average build and about the same age, boomers in our prime.

Shuttleworth moves closer and I extend my hand. "Nice to meet you, John. What a beautiful boat."

"Thanks. Ted said you flew in from the Canaries."

That puts a smile on my face. "Yeah, I took the scenic route."

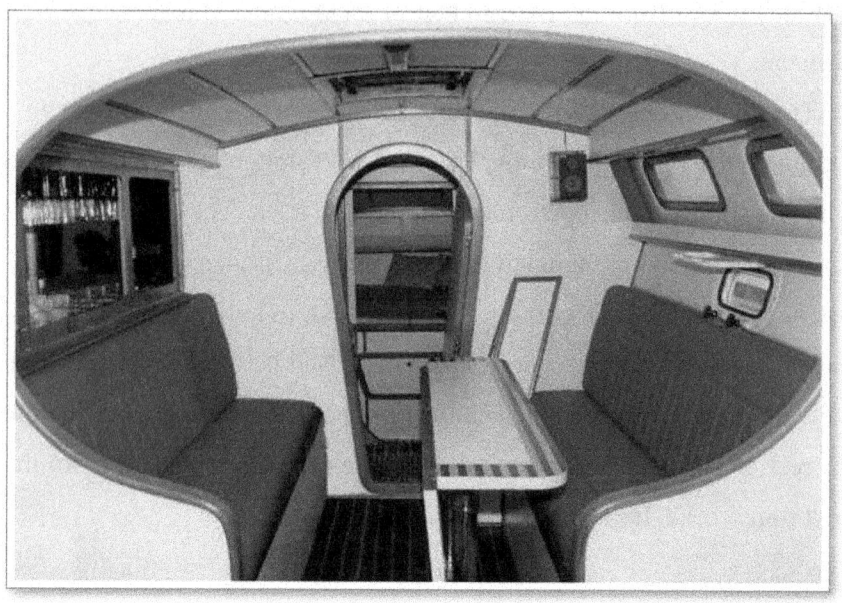

Spectrum-42 main salon on starboard, looking forward from the galley

For the rest of the day, we keep busy finishing minor repairs, loading groceries, and getting shipshape. In the evening, we all get together in the main salon forward of the galley for a light meal to discuss the new plan. Shuttleworth explains the details of his inspection and says the boat remains in great shape, ready to sail, even after the unplanned stress test during the storm.

"What about the rudder?" I ask because he didn't mention it.

Shuttleworth's reply comes as a surprise. "Most sailboats steer with one rudder. Why not *Toucan*?" By *most* he's referring to the typical monohull sailboats which far outnumber the catamarans and trimarans. He says a replacement rudder can be fabricated after we arrive in the Canary Islands.

Captain Ted raises an eyebrow and glances at Joni to gauge her reaction. I keep quiet and pick up my beer bottle for another sip. To convince the group of his certainty, Shuttleworth agrees to sail as crew, at least as far as the Canaries. When Ted hears that the designer is willing to stake his reputation on the proposal, he sits up straight, lifts his glass, and says, "Welcome aboard."

Ted takes a sip of his drink then adds, "If you're going to fly home from the Canaries, do you happen to know anyone who can sail the Atlantic with us?"

"Quite possibly. I'll make a few phone calls this evening."

Before retiring for the night, Joni walks up the ramp to the club and removes the "Crew Wanted" notice from the bulletin board. When she returns, Shuttleworth is arranging his things in the main salon on starboard. She parks herself next to me on the bench in the cockpit and runs her fingers through her hair.

She leans over and whispers, "I didn't like posting that notice in the first place. It's a relief to have Shuttleworth along for the trip."

"I agree. We sure as hell don't want some talkative know-it-all onboard boasting nonstop about who-knows-what."

"Or worse," Joni adds with a grimace.

***

Lying in my bunk in the aft cabin, I feel uneasy about the more important issue. To me it seems unsafe to sail a thousand miles for a week or more with an impaired vessel. It would be no big deal in fair weather but steering a wide catamaran in rough weather could place undue stress on a single rudder.

With smaller catamarans, like my old Hobie Cat, each rudder has been built strong enough to steer the boat on its own. It actually sails quite often with one hull raised out of the water.

Of course, Shuttleworth is intimately familiar with his design and supervised the construction of *Toucan* at every step. But still, he designed the catamaran from the get-go to sail with two rudders. So, what's the big hurry? Now I'm thinking we should find a translator and have a new rudder fabricated right here in La Coruña with easy access to far better resources than on a tourist island in the Canaries.

I roll onto my side and look through the clear Plexiglas of the escape hatch across the surface of the water to the other hull, the one with no rudder. Frustrated, I toss and turn as the sound of wire rope halyards slapping against hollow aluminum masts rings out of tune.

***

Still restless at dawn's first light, I slip out of my bunk and walk up the ramp to the seawall. A lone seabird dips its wingtips from side to side almost touching the water as it skims across the harbor. Pacing back and forth, thinking about how I'd feel if I don't go. What if the other rudder breaks off while they're underway? If I choose not to go, I'd definitely regret not being onboard to help. So, my mind's made up and I return to the boat.

The inspection is nearly complete. Ted holds the hatch cover open as Shuttleworth emerges from the engine compartment and signals his approval. Joni climbs into the cockpit a moment later and suggests we all venture into town for breakfast.

The oldest section of the city, the Cidade Vella, is just a short walk from the yacht club. The balconies on every floor of the buildings facing the waterfront are closed in with glazed windows as a protection against the notorious rainy weather that often blows in from the North Atlantic.

Within a few blocks, Joni selects a lively restaurant on Rúa Real. The discussion at the table soon focuses on taking care of last-minute details on the boat, such as topping off the tanks with freshwater and diesel fuel.

The waiter refills our cups with hot coffee. Ted adds a splash of cream to his and says, "I heard good news this morning on BBC Radio. They're predicting clear skies and fair winds for the next two days."

Joni says, "It's about time."

Uncle Jim, quiet and reserved, has only one question. "Are we stopping along the way, maybe in Lisbon or Casablanca?"

That's exactly what I wondered about yesterday. The answer is always the same—not enough time. Jeez, I could easily spend a week or more right here exploring La Coruña and even Galicia.

All eyes turn to Captain Ted. "No, we're sailing straight to the Canaries."

"And don't worry," says Joni. "There's enough food onboard for a week or more."

The positive energy of the group feels right, and there's no need to bring up the subject of the rudder. Driven by my commitment to the task and the age-old desire for adventure, my decision has already been made.

Damn straight I'm going.

As we're getting ready to leave the restaurant, Shuttleworth delivers some comforting news. "Last night when I called a friend of mine, he said he's interested in sailing with you to Florida but will need help with the expenses."

"We'll take care of that," says Ted with a wave of his hand.

"I'll let him know," says John.

On the way out, Joni interrupts Ted at the checkout counter and adds half a dozen powdered croissants to the tab. For safekeeping, the box of goodies goes with me.

Ted stops at the dockmaster's office to settle up for the fees and Joni leads the way as we walk down the ramp to the boat in single file.

Shuttleworth and I start preparing for departure.

When Ted arrives, he says, "If the water tanks are full, let's disconnect the hose." He never yells or shouts. Most of the time it sounds like he's reviewing a checklist. As he climbs aboard, he reminds us. "Be sure to unplug the cord from the electrical post."

The midday Sun has warmed the morning breeze and Shuttleworth is in high spirits. "What a great day for sailing!"

I'm excited about finally untying from the dock and mumble a short prayer to the wind gods for a whole week of fair weather. Hope they're listening.

 ## The Canary Current

The dockmaster's assistant unwraps the stern line from the cleat and tosses it to me. Shuttleworth has already cast off *Toucan's* bow lines and, with all free and clear, signals the captain. We bring the fenders in, coil the dock lines, and drop them in the locker. Some of the boaters in the marina are rubbernecking as Ted motors the sleek new catamaran toward open water. Joni and Uncle Jim wave farewell to La Coruña.

When we clear the breakwater with plenty of room to maneuver, Ted idles into the wind so I can hoist the mainsail. Once the sail reaches its full height, Joni turns the winch to tighten it. Ted shuts off the engine and tilts the propeller housing out of the water with its electric motor. I lower the leeward daggerboard to minimize the boat's slippage sideways while under sail. Shuttleworth loosens the line to unfurl the genoa, and Joni cranks the winch to bring it in. The skipper turns the bows off the wind, just enough to fill the sails, and the springtime breeze from the northwest launches the catamaran into the North Atlantic.

Shuttleworth moves over to the windward side of the boat by the daggerboard and motions for me to join him. We stand with our backs to the wind, facing the sails, his long hair blowing forward.

He says, "Looks like the mainsail and the genny survived the storm last week without being ripped to shreds."

Holding one hand on the shroud, I lean back to see the top of the mainsail. "Yeah, the sailmaker would be proud."

His comment about the mainsail reminds me of our sailing club in St. Pete. "When we get back to Florida, *Toucan* will join the racing fleet, so I'll need to come up with a handicap rating."

Shuttleworth says, "You'll need to take some measurements."

"I've got the easy ones. Do you happen to know the sail areas, preferably in square feet?"

Of course he does. He's the boat designer.

"Sure, the main is 620 and the genny is 470." He pauses because Captain Ted is looking our way. "Let's talk more about the rating formula after things settle down."

"Okay, I'll have plenty of time to get the other measurements."

From the helm the captain hollers, "I've got some telltales in my bag. Ask Joni to get 'em for you."

Both sails need a simple added touch to aid in the task of trimming them for optimum performance. I attach a set of bright orange, six-inch ribbons to each sail about two feet back from the leading edges, as high as I can reach, so the helmsman can see how the wind flows across the sails. Other ribbons can be attached when the sails come down. If the helmsman can get the telltales flying straight back, by changing course ever so slightly, then the sails will be trimmed properly.

There's something special about adjusting the shape of the sails to take full advantage of the wind's power. It's like a nonstop struggle with two elements of nature, the wind and the water, a constant challenge to keep the boat moving across the surface but not so fast you lose control.

Toucan heads south along the Iberian coast with sailing conditions near perfect. Cirrus clouds, a mild chop, and the wind speed at fifteen knots on the aft quarter all make for a pleasant ride. There's no place I'd rather be.

***

By sunset of the first day, we have sailed on a broad reach south of the landmark at Cape Finisterre with its prominent lighthouse still in view. The Romans named this point of land from the Latin, *finis terrae,* because they believed it marked the end of the known world.

Standing in the companionway, half in the cabin and half out, I watch Ted at the chart table as he fusses with one of the latest navigational systems on the market, the satnav. We're both fascinated with the idea of using satellites for navigation, no longer having to depend on signals from land-based towers. He draws circles and arrows on the chart to indicate the boat's heading with the date and time noted next to each.

I step back into the cockpit next to the winch with the telltales in view. Ted joins us and takes a seat on the bench next to Joni.

"We just received an update to our position."

She says, "I'm curious. How often can we get a fix from the satellites?"

"It could be hours between fixes," says Ted. "The satnav needs to receive signals from four satellites at the same time to compute our location, and there's only ten in orbit right now."

It's amazing technology. In the near future, as more satellites are added to the system, they say we'll be able to get an accurate fix any time of day, even far offshore.

"What's our next waypoint?" asks Shuttleworth as he steers casually, one hand on the helm with a joy that's hard to hide.

"We're headed for a position farther offshore in the Canary Current. Hold it at one-ninety for now," says Captain Ted.

"Ah, yes, the Canary Current," says Shuttleworth. "It's wide and strong enough to give us a boost in the right direction."

At the end of the Gulf Stream, the ocean currents form a broad, shallow, slower-moving stream called the North Atlantic Drift. Part of it branches to the south like a river in the ocean, flowing along the coast of Portugal to join the wind-driven Canary Current.

Hours later, Ted checks our position and wants to change course, which will put the wind directly astern. That calls for the spinnaker. Joni takes the helm from Shuttleworth and steers the catamaran with ease. John and I spring into action. We quickly furl the genoa on the forestay and lower the mainsail. Joni turns the wheel until she feels the wind directly behind us and keeps an eye on the wave action.

Ted hollers up from the nav station. "That's good. Keep it there at one-eighty." The wind direction is still in our favor.

The area forward of the mast has a dark webbing stretched tight between the hulls—the trampoline. It's strong enough to jump on when changing sails. I jerk the bag with the spinnaker out of the sail locker and toss it on the tramp. The head of the sail gets shackled to the halyard first, then the two trim lines, called sheets, to the corners. The skipper gives the signal, and I hoist the sail while Shuttleworth trims it. The spinnaker balloons out in front of the boat, and the wrinkles in the lightweight sail cloth fade fast.

We don't want the daggerboards dragging in the water while sailing downwind. They're over eight feet tall and so heavy that a pulley system attached to a winch is needed to lift them. They slide up and down in watertight trunks built amidships in each hull. Since we're not in any big hurry, I take my time and grind the winches to raise the boards one at a time, up to a mark drawn on each. Now they're inside the trunks, not dragging in the water.

When I return to the cockpit and sit next to Ted, he's watching the spinnaker sway gently in the breeze. He looks quite satisfied.

"Captain, what's the size of your spinnaker?" Ted likes it when I call him captain or refer to him as the skipper.

He says, "The British sailmaker measured it at fourteen hundred square feet."

Shuttleworth glances forward. "It's a work of art with that multi-colored toucan."

***

Shortly after the Sun dips below the horizon, Venus brightens and soon follows. *Toucan* sails gracefully into the darkness across the choppy sea while floating downstream on the river in the ocean: a beautiful evening. We split up into two teams, Ted and Joni on deck for four hours, then Shuttleworth and me. The team down below tries to sleep or eat while the team on deck focuses constantly on steering dead downwind. Any one of us can steer, but the teams have leaders. Joni assists Ted. Shuttleworth takes pleasure in sailing his new design. My job, for now, is to keep the spinnaker trimmed, quite easy with these favorable conditions.

Toucan's spinnaker.

Just after the 8 p.m. shift change, I update our location in the ship's logbook. Yawning, ready for a nap, I sit on the edge of my bunk, slip off the stinky brown Top-Siders without untying them, and lean back. The lower edge of the escape hatch lines up with the top of the mattress cushion. Supposedly, if the boat flips over, the hatch will still be above the waterline. When I gaze out, it's like looking into one of those extra-large machines at the laundromat during the wash cycle.

***

Joni hollers at Shuttleworth in the main salon and nudges my foot as she passes my bunk. It must be midnight already. Ted waits at the helm for us guys to take over, and once we get our bearings, he ducks down below to catch some Zs with Joni. Shuttleworth steers while I prepare two cups of coffee in the dim galley. Can't find the croissants.

John takes a sip of the fresh brew. "Thanks." He pauses for a minute or so. "Have you measured the J-dimension yet?"

"Yeah, it's seventeen feet from the base of the mast out to the bottom of the forestay."

In sailboat racing there needs to be a handicap rating rule to determine the winners, unless all the boats in the race are of the same design and size, same make and model. Otherwise, the fast boats would always win. It'd be the same with automobiles. Why enter a race with an old stock car against a new Ferrari?

I swirl the coffee in my tumbler and take a sip. "Our sailing club in Florida needed a rating system too. When we contacted the local yacht clubs about racing with their monohull fleets, they agreed to create a separate division for catamarans and trimarans only if we had a handicap system to determine the winners. So, we started testing your rating rule."

"Are you still using that basic formula?" asks John.

"We did at first but quickly found that we needed to separate the cruising boats from the lightweight racers. So, we created a cruising fleet for the heavy trimarans like the Cross- and Brown-designs and a racing division for the faster boats like the Sarasota Stilettos. That didn't work too well either, so we cranked a performance coefficient into the formula. As we gathered more race data on each boat, we fine-tuned its rating, and ended up with a performance-based handicap system."

"How's it working?" asks John. "Getting any complaints?"

"A few, but overall, it works." I finish my coffee. "It's far from an exact science—too many unmeasurable variables. When I get back to my computer, I'll calculate a handicap rating for *Toucan*."

"I suppose you start with a performance coefficient of one point zero and adjust it up or down after a couple of good races," says John.

"Exactly, and with *Toucan* the only thing unmeasured is the weight. We'll hook up a scale when it's hauled out of the water."

"It weighed about twelve thousand pounds when we launched it."

"I'll start with that."

"It sounds like you're the one adjusting all the ratings."

"Mostly, the race data dictates the changes. But we get feedback from the sailors too. It's a numbers game. The program I wrote based on your formula cranks out the ratings, and I merely keep a close watch for anomalies."

"Such as?" queries John.

"Let's say a boat is forced into irons during a race and spends a few minutes in recovery. Or the spinnaker gets all tangled up while the crew brings it down. It wouldn't be fair to adjust their rating because they sailed poorly in one race."

"That would give them an advantage on corrected time in the next race," says the boat designer. "And you only consider changing a boat's coefficient when the race data supports it?"

"That's the ideal situation. With the racing fleet, it's easier because they compete often and sail well. The sailors in the cruising division don't show up regularly and seem to care more about enjoying the weather. They're not so competitive."

As *Toucan* charges south in the dark, I place the empty tumblers on the top step leading to the galley.

John continues to steer the boat downwind. "How's the turnout for the races?"

"It's getting better every year. Last Memorial Day weekend, forty-five multihulls competed in the fifth annual Round Egmont Race in the mouth of Tampa Bay."

"Unfortunately, the final turning mark of the course floated away before the leaders could round it and the race committee had to abandon the race."

"Did you say the mark floated away?"

"Yeah, it was one of those large orange, inflatable buoys and the volunteers who placed it in the deep water didn't anchor it properly."

"What a bummer! The anchor probably never reached the bottom."

***

Another four-hour watch ends at four o'clock in the morning, and I holler into the captain's cabin, "It's time."

Ten minutes after Ted takes the helm with Joni at his side, John zonks out in the main salon on starboard. I climb down below and fall back into my bunk. When Ted starts the engine about four hours later, the rumbling sounds the alarm for the next shift change. Didn't I just doze off? I pull on my jacket and climb back up into the cockpit.

Uncle Jim stayed in his cabin all night and developed a case of seasickness, the mean, nasty effect of agitation with the gentle rocking of the boat. He pops his aching head up through the companionway when he hears the engine. "Are we pulling into port?"

"Not yet," says Ted. "We need to run the engine twice a day to keep the batteries charged."

Seriously afflicted, the poor bloke backs down and turns aft toward the head. The sad sounds of Uncle Jim puking his guts out, moaning, and barfing some more makes me cringe. All of us have experienced seasickness at some point and we sympathize with him. It's a drag.

"I think the diesel fumes must have set him off."

Ted scoots over so I can take the helm. "After the retched dry-heaves he'll acclimate faster on an empty stomach."

"I wish there was something we could do for him."

"So do I," says Ted. "Last night Joni told me that he was in the military during WWII. Said he was captured and tortured by the enemy."

"Oh no! That's terrible. Where?"

"Somewhere in the Far East."

The other day when Uncle Jim first showed up on the dock his aloofness came across as unfriendly. Was he uncertain about being confined to a small boat for weeks at a time? Maybe that was part of it but now I find out he's not just a war veteran. He was held prisoner. Damn. Sad news.

It's been nearly twenty years since my tours in Vietnam. Most of my duty was spent at a base camp, working as an official postal clerk handling mail for about three hundred soldiers. I drove the same jeep every day, delivering outgoing mail to the post office and picking up bags of incoming letters and packages.

Nobody messed with the mailman. That's one of the reasons I stayed twice as long as most guys. I got lucky—never set foot in the jungle.

But for three of my hometown friends, it was quite the opposite. They went through hell in the thick of it, serving with infantry and artillery squads. For what?

Hoff is one of them. The war in the jungle changed him. Like Uncle Jim, they'll suffer for the rest of their lives with terrible memories. Ted is quiet. Neither of us knows what to do or say—we're both lost in our own thoughts.

Several minutes pass in silence.

"Maybe he'll feel better in the morning. Are you doin' okay?"

Ted looks up at the clouds. "I'm fine, but this weather's got me worried."

"At least it's not blowin' out of the south." I pull a seat cushion under my butt and check the sails. The trim lines from the lower corners of the spinnaker are stretched too tight. If the wind picks up much more, the sail will need to come down.

I nudge Ted on the arm. "Go ahead and get some rest."

He shuts off the engine and retreats to his cabin to snuggle up with Joni in their cozy v-berth.

Minutes later from the starboard side, Shuttleworth emerges halfway from the galley with two croissants wrapped in paper towels and places them on the bench next to the companionway. He glances at me with a boyish grin, disappears, then returns with two cups of steaming coffee. One of us has to steer so he slides my croissant within reach. Wow, it's powdered on top and stuffed with a creamy almond filling. Careful it doesn't squirt out the other end.

A great way to start another four-hour shift. Too good to be true.

***

Unbeknownst to us, at this very moment, back at the yacht club in La Coruña—now hundreds of miles to the north—the barometric pressure has dropped quickly and ushered in rough weather with strong wind, thunder, and lightning. Most of the boaters have returned to the safety of the marina and a few stragglers are still coming in. No one is venturing out. The club burgee has been lowered and the red flags signaling extreme weather are snapping in the wind.

As the storm advances to the south, it will soon catch up with the catamaran.

 ## Riding the Storm

"Being at the time rather 'hippie' minded, Conrad had some vague idea about man's position in nature, but as yet he had no inkling of the awful struggle which must be maintained when man pits himself against the natural forces of wind and water; nor did he yet know the great rewards, the sense of achievement, the beauty and the joy, the pure hymn of the oceans."

(Tristan Jones, *The Incredible Voyage*, 1977)

The wind strengthens, still from the north, and pushes the waves higher. All throughout the day under overcast skies, *Toucan* runs with the storm. Ted stands at the helm and steers the boat straight downwind. He looks tired.

It's starting to rain. We need to drop the spinnaker. We're already dressed to the hilt in foul weather gear, so we team up to bring it down. John slowly releases the halyard while Joni and I gather and stuff the wet sail in the bag.

The mainsail alone now propels the boat over the waves. It's tied out nearly perpendicular to the wind and held down with a block and tackle attached to the end of the boom. All the hatch covers and the sliding tops above both companionways are closed tight against the rainfall.

The unsteady motion of the boat and the limited workspace in the galley challenge more than Joni's culinary skills. She dances to maintain her balance and to prevent accidents. She makes sure nothing goes unattended unless properly secured. No glass containers allowed. We'd never find all the broken pieces.

Under normal conditions the gimbaled stovetop remains level and the steel rails an inch high prevent pots and pans from sliding off. Not today. The boat rocks too much to fix a decent meal. Even so, Joni manages to prepare sandwiches and drinks before darkness falls.

We take turns eating in the main salon and after receiving a round of thanks for supper, Joni says, "You guys know where the goodies are. Help yourselves. And you should eat the fruit before it goes bad."

We finished the second bag of tortilla chips yesterday, so John works on an orange with his thumbnail and flicks another piece of peel over the side. I down the last swig of my apple juice, squeeze the air out of the plastic bottle, and twist the cap on tight.

Oftentimes when boaters are far offshore and need to relieve their bladders, the guys simply take a leak over the side or off the stern. But for the duration of this storm, we agree to use the head and not run the risk of somebody falling overboard with their zipper down.

Joni and Ted share a private head located forward of the center cabin adjacent to their sleeping quarters. With my bunk also on port, I need to climb up and cross over the cockpit then go down into the starboard hull to the other head, about the size of a short Porta Potty, behind the galley in the aft section.

Forward of the galley, through the main salon, a door leads into a closet compartment with a tiny sink and a hose with a shower head. There's nothing in there that can't get wet. Continuing forward still, another door leads into Uncle Jim's private quarters. Rainwater drips from the corner of the hatchway built into the ceiling like a skylight, but only enough to keep his bedding damp.

Uncle Jim can't be much help on deck, so he stays down below. That's part of why he's seasick. Every time he finishes barking at the porcelain, he returns to his bunk in the darkness. The roar of the fiberglass hull crashing into the waves and the howling of the wind echoing nonstop in his cabin does not help his condition.

Up on deck the tasks are demanding as the teams trade shifts, monitor the satnav, and wrestle with the helm all through the stormy night. It's getting near dawn, and we're surrounded by towering waves with occasional silver-white spindrifts.

Uncle Jim holds tight with both hands as he appears in the companionway at the most inopportune moment. Just as he looks forward, spray from a wave top drenches his upper body. He shakes it off, embarrassed and scared. His wide eyes show it as he backs down into the cabin.

***

Ready for another shift change, John reminds me to wake up Ted and Joni. None of us are getting enough sleep. I climb down clutching the handrail and knock on their cabin door. A sleepy response makes it through the roar.

"Already?"

Ted comes out first and scoots behind me at the chart table. He slides open the top portion of the companionway to get a feel for the weather. As expected, it's still overcast but the rain has slowed to a drizzle. He struggles into his foul weather gear and climbs into the cockpit.

"Mornin'," he mumbles. After a moment, he adds, "We've logged quite a few sea miles during the night."

At the helm John pushes his hood back. "Probably set a record that'll be hard to beat. Have we passed Cabo da Roca yet?"

The rocky cliff promontory and lighthouse mark the westernmost extent of mainland Portugal and continental Europe, not Cape Finisterre like the Romans believed.

I hear John's question and step into the cockpit. "Yes, we're about a hundred and twenty miles west of it and a bit south."

Once Joni arrives on deck, Captain Ted makes an announcement.

"We need to agree on the immediate actions to take in case someone falls overboard."

"Hey guys, it ain't gonna happen," says Joni. "Nobody's fallin' overboard."

John responds with a grin and a wink. "If it's me, throw over a flask of rum and keep sailing."

Does John believe, like I do, that a rescue would be nearly impossible in a storm like this? The waves are too big.

Ted draws our attention again by clearing his throat, his distinctive habit, and directs his comments at John since the two of them have never sailed together. "Here's the plan."

He then looks at me. "If Shuttleworth happens to go over, you start hollering to wake Joni and me and at the same time throw a seat cushion over the stern. Throw the ring buoy, a life vest, anything that floats to help find our way back."

"If Shuttleworth's in the water, I'll jump in and save him."

The captain pauses, exhales, and scratches behind his ear. "Will you two stop joking? This is serious." He sounds on edge, frustrated.

We're all experienced sailors and know the man overboard recovery procedure. Captain Ted is right, though; the situation is getting serious. Considering the boat's speed and the amount of time it would take to lower the sail, start the motor, and drive the boat back into these waves, the person in the water would be hard to find even in daylight, highly unlikely at night.

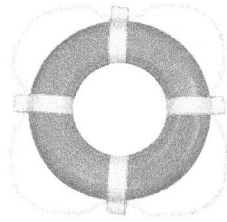

"If John falls overboard, I definitely won't jump in to save him. I won't even be able to let go of the helm. And yeah, I'll start yelling like hell."

Joni says, "I'll take the helm from you as soon as I can."

Ted continues. "We're talking about what needs to be done, not about who does it. Most importantly, we'll need to keep the victim in sight. Then, as soon as possible, record the coordinates and time of day on the chart, and make the initial Mayday distress call."

Joni shakes her head. "We'll never get any response in this storm."

"Probably not, but we'll make the call anyway."

Another vessel may be nearby, and maritime law requires them to lend assistance.

"Then with three of us on deck we'll bring down the mainsail."

He takes a deep breath, probably reflecting on the grim possibility of somebody falling overboard, "and start the engine. Uncle Jim could help by monitoring the radio."

Then nobody says anything. I stare at the raindrops splashing on the deck. Ted lowers his head and starts for the companionway. Joni turns to Shuttleworth when he speaks.

"Hey, I'm still here and we're sailing to the Canaries."

***

The storm continues to strengthen and demands our constant attention. Often hours pass without a word being said. Are the waves growing taller, maybe reaching as high as twenty feet? It's hard to tell.

The fourth day presents a nonstop survival challenge. Staying calm and focused plays a major role in steering the speeding catamaran, which constantly seems to be right on the edge of flipping over. The situation borders on insane and forces us to confront our limitations.

We adapt to the harsh environment as best we can as our bodies move in harmony with the boat. At times, for maybe ten exciting seconds, *Toucan* dances in sync, balanced with the rhythm of the stormy sea, then continues stumbling through, jerking forward and sideways like a roller coaster.

Ted can't sleep so he stays on deck. He adjusts the hood of his jacket and glances up at the full mainsail. "I'll take the helm while you two shorten the main. Put in a double reef."

"Good idea," says John.

The sailmakers did an excellent job with the mainsail. Metal grommets called reef points were sewn in so the sail can be shortened.

John goes forward to the mast and unwraps the halyard from the winch.

He hollers, "Okay, ready."

I position the traveler in the center of the cockpit, tighten the mainsheet, and loosen the outhaul—the line that secures the foot of the sail tight along the boom. I brush the rain off my face and nod to John signaling him to release the downhaul line that keeps the sail taut along the mast.

With the strong wind against the sail, both of us need to pull down hard on the luff until the downhaul hook can be attached to the upper grommet. John winches the sail lower and we then gather and tie the bottom section around the boom.

We take a short break then get back at it.

John cranks the halyard winch to tighten the luff. I adjust the outhaul, then loosen the traveler and mainsheet to allow the shortened sail to return to its position perpendicular to the wind. We fasten another line from the end of the boom to a stainless padeye on deck to hold the sail down and out.

Our catamaran now resembles a wide raft with one small sail driving the boat southward. All the while, Ted maintains the boat's downwind direction, aligning it with the wind and waves.

As I creep back to the cockpit, one of the seat cushions gets blown overboard too quick to catch.

Ted shouts, "Forget it. No way we can turn around. Let's toss the other ones in a locker. Clear everything off the deck."

We've reached the point of no return. The storm and the rough seas now prevent us from sailing safely in any direction except with the wind, straight to the Canaries.

***

I scoot along the bench toward the companionway and lean in to see the clock over the nav station. I holler into the captain's quarters for Joni, "It's that time again."

She steps into the center cabin, drags a wide-toothed comb across her head, and squints up at me. "Okay, I'm up but maybe not awake." She wiggles the comb to undo a knot.

Ted turns the helm over to John and climbs down below. I need to update our position on the chart, so I follow him.

He asks Joni, "Where'd we stash the movie camera?"

Joni lifts her wet jacket off the hook and slips it on over her damp jersey. "You're not gonna take the camera out there, are you?" She's still groggy from a restless slumber.

"It'll only take a few minutes. I want to get some footage of Shuttleworth at the helm with these big waves in the background before it starts raining again."

Joni sighs. "Look under the chart table."

Ted retrieves the camera, braces himself against the countertop, and inserts a blank VHS cassette. Needing both hands to step up into the cockpit, he slides his right hand through the cord to dangle the camera from his wrist and climbs up. I move the empty cassette case off the chart and go back out.

Holding tight on the top step in the companionway, Joni says, "Ted, be careful." She draws in a frustrated breath.

We all fear the real possibility of launching into a comedy of errors—somebody trips and falls in the cockpit, the distracted helmsman tries to assist, the boat veers off course out of control and flips over. We'd be lost at sea.

Ted motions to me. "Come up by the mast with me. We're gonna make a movie."

I steady myself by moving forward from one handhold to the next. Holy shit! This is almost like trying to stand up in a raft while shooting the rapids. With my right arm wrapped around the mast, I hold tight with my left hand to the strap on the back of Ted's safety harness. For a future audience, the camera captures a blurry and jerky moment of the storm with Shuttleworth casually steering one-handed, attempting to appear relaxed, while the monstrous waves behind him rise to the occasion.

The storm isn't letting up, not by any stretch. The constant, strong wind has pushed the waves to great heights, and although the wind speed varies, the waves roll at a steady pace. With the reefed mainsail still up, the boat reacts to the wind and at times sails faster than the waves, sometimes slower. On top of a wave, I can peer down into the valley between crests. Astern, the top of the wave appears as high as a house. As a Florida sailor, I have never seen anything like it. Shuttleworth stays calm and acts like these monster waves are normal on his side of the Atlantic.

***

Toward the end of the evening shift on day four, more than halfway to the Canaries, I finally feel acclimated to the unfavorable conditions. We have endured gloomy overcast skies for days with everything wet or damp and the nonstop rocking motion has turned my sea legs into storm legs. It's strange how humans have the astounding ability to adapt to their environment.

Forecasters use terms like "angry seas," "confused seas," and "gale force winds" to define heavy weather conditions but those don't apply to this storm. Yes, the waves have grown tall, but they aren't breaking like the ones surfers ride in Hawaii. The waves don't roll in a gentle fashion, but predictably one after the other.

We're traveling faster than the waves, up and over. When the boat charges into the back of the next wave, the bow lights disappear, and we get another taste of a saltwater shower flashing into the cockpit. At least it's not freezing cold. At this pace we'll arrive in a warm subtropical climate in a few more days.

This demanding situation reminds me of the popular '70s tune by The Doors: "Riders on the Storm." I make a mental note to pop that cassette into my Walkman when things settle down.

As the rain starts and stops, we tighten or loosen the drawstrings on our hoods. The wind lets up a bit, then strengthens again, always above twenty-five knots but never in the gale force range above forty. The storm is not about to pass over, and we will not be sailing out from under it. Fortunately, the wind direction stays steady, pushing us right where we want to go.

Both teams know the importance of holding a proper course. This morning as a safety precaution, we double-tied the boom out to the port side so it can't accidentally swing across the cockpit. We rehearsed the procedure to follow if the wind, as strong as it is, fills the mainsail from the opposite side. That could happen if the boat drifts off course too much to port or, less likely, with a sudden shift in the wind direction. The forceful change would cause undue stress on the sail, the rigging, and the single rudder. The helmsman would then need to wrestle with the wheel to bring the boat back on course. Drifting too much in the other direction, to starboard, would require an easier adjustment back downwind.

Toucan's bows flare out above the waterline to add buoyancy in situations like this. Still, when the catamaran starts to surf down the front of a wave, the helmsman has to be careful not to let the increase in speed bury the bows too deep into the backside of a wave. With the reefed mainsail secured out to port, he can turn to the right, sail through the valley, then back downwind, never allowing the boat to turn sideways to the wind.

Whatever caused the rudder to break away last week could just as easily happen today, at any minute. But that's life. There's only one way out of this storm and being fearful about it won't help a bit. Just go with it. Shuttleworth reveals no sense of apprehension and beyond his concentration, there's not a sliver of concern. About halfway through the afternoon watch, I stretch and voice my uneasiness. "What if we do flip this thing?"

Steering with caution, John glances out to sea. "There may be a wave out here that could overwhelm us, but we haven't seen it yet."

If *Toucan's* inventory included an emergency sea drogue, we could drag it through the water to slow the boat and minimize the risk of a capsize. But since it doesn't, we could rig up a bridle off the stern cleats and drag the anchor chain behind us.

I harbor my own ideas about the dangers we face but want to make sure I'm not forgetting something.

"Hey John, what's your plan if the wind strengthens to gale force and these waves start crashing into the cockpit?" I rub the back of my neck.

The British boat designer says, in his calm matter-of-fact way, "We'll bring down the reefed mainsail, start the engine, and motor sideways to the waves with the windward daggerboard cranked all the way down."

"Oh right, the daggerboard wild card tactic. I love your confident, positive attitude. Seriously, it's the best way to live."

I pause and say with a grin of amusement. "And what if we lose the other rudder?"

"Take a break mate, it ain't gonna happen."

***

The storm dies a slow death during the fourth night. A slice of pink sky lightens the gray clouds on the eastern horizon and the sea begins to settle down. John was right. The single rudder has indeed held tight through the ordeal. We made it and I've fallen in love with *Toucan*.

The satisfaction of sailing with the storm puts us in a philosophical mood and our predawn conversation drifts toward a somewhat serious discussion of the meaning of life. John relaxes at the helm with his jacket unzipped. I stand up in the cockpit without having to hold on and rotate my shoulders to loosen up.

"So, let's each summarize in three words or less."

"Summarize what?" John asks. "The meaning of life?"

"Yeah, like, 'Do unto others' or maybe 'Praise the Lord.'"

John says, "How about, 'Know yourself,' 'Follow your bliss,' and 'Be here now'?"

"Don't forget, 'Go placidly' and 'Seek Nirvana.'"

John smiles while removing his jacket.

I admit to being wide open on the subject and make a confession. "Sometimes I feel like a passenger on a bus with a bunch of other bozos, each with different ideas about where we're going and how to get there."

The Englishman waves his hand across his face and summarizes his version in three words. "Let's go sailing."

So, we shake out the reef in the mainsail, unfurl the genoa, and adjust our course to take full advantage of the light breeze, keeping the telltales flying straight back.

Toucan sails into the predawn light with only the sound of the twin hulls slicing through the mild chop. Ted and Joni climb into the cockpit carrying their jackets and look around. The sunrise is visible again. And without jumping up and down, applauding, or even mentioning it, we privately celebrate a new beginning.

***

We drape our foul weather gear over the lifelines and brace the hatch covers open to air out the cabins. Joni finds a sunny spot on the tramp to dry her beach towel, then takes the helm from Shuttleworth. Exhausted, he goes below to catch an overdue nap. Ted eases the line on the winch to lower the leeward daggerboard then trolls his favorite fishing lure, a silver spoon, off the stern hoping to hook a fresh, aquatic delicacy for lunch.

Uncle Jim emerges from his cabin and stands on the lower step of the companionway, bracing himself with both hands. Every white hair on his head glows in the sunlight. His face still ghostly, he forces a smile and asks Joni, "Is this what you call smooth sailing?"

When Joni turns, the Sun lights up her face and she squints. "Yessirree, and it should stay like this for the rest of the trip."

He steps into the cockpit and takes a seat. "Where are we?"

The nearest island is subtropical Madeira, nicknamed *Pearl of the Atlantic*. It belongs to Portugal, and we passed due east of it earlier. He probably prefers that Joni answer but I'm certain of our location.

"We're about a hundred twenty nautical miles east of Madeira. And it's more than a day's sail to the Canaries."

Uncle Jim glances to the west then astern at Ted's fishing line. He doesn't say anything so maybe he's still feeling queasy.

Now that our shift is over, John and I can get some rest. But first, I jump down into the cabin and search through the Tupperware box for 'The Doors' tape. I grab the L.A. Woman cassette and load it into the silver and blue player clipped to my waistband. Crashing on the tramp looks good. I plop down in a shady spot, adjust the headphones, fast-forward to the last song on Side B, press play, and lean back against the crossbeam knowing I'll probably doze off before the best part, the keyboard solo.

***

Mid-morning on day six all hands are on deck basking in the sunshine sparkling off the water. A light breeze fills in from the north, so we retrieve the wet spinnaker from the locker and hoist it up to dry.

The mountaintops of Tenerife appear first, then the rugged, steep shoreline, bathed in the morning light. Such a beautiful sight: a reward for making it through the storm. Seabirds plummet straight down from great heights and plunge into the water to catch their prey.

As we sail within a few miles of the northeast shore, two homing pigeons land on deck. Not surprisingly, they have ID tags banded on both legs. It's fascinating how they can fly for so many miles, targeting a specific destination with mysterious navigational skills.

Joni says, "Don't chase 'em off. Let's see what they do."

The birds soon settle in a corner on the bench. They're taking a break, quite relaxed, and don't seem bothered as we move about in the cockpit. Joni fills a saucer with water.

I scoot closer to our feathered friends. "I'd like see what's on the tags."

John agrees, "Let's have a look." He grabs 'em, one at a time, and with Joni's help reads the info on the tags while I take notes on a scrap of paper. The blue tags on the right legs are labeled PORT85, possibly identifying the Portuguese owner who registered the birds last year. The reason for the pink and red tags on the left legs is still up in the air.

The pigeons refuse to drink from the unfamiliar container, so Joni splashes the water in the deep saucer with her fingers. They've heard that refreshing sound at home since birth, and soon take a long drink. Homing pigeons are incredibly smart, and Joni knows her birds.

After a while, John chases them off the boat forcing them to continue their mission—flying home. I transfer the info from the leg bands to the logbook in case we come across someone in the Canaries who seems interested.

***

When we get closer to the island, I point toward the cliff. "See that road halfway up the mountain?"

Ted says, "I see a guardrail."

"That's where I parked and watched for you last week."

Joni and John adjust the sails while I tell the story about *Señor* Doorman at the yacht club.

Ted expresses a genuine concern, "We weren't sure if we'd be able to get in touch with you."

"My plan was to wait two weeks before giving up."

John tightens the genoa and looks over his shoulder, "Not a bad place to hang out."

"One of the best." I pause and smile. "Maria, the lady who works at the front desk of the hotel, kept talking about an upcoming celebration with parades and parties. Something about the Canaries becoming independent from Spain."

I glance back at the guardrail. "She's taking an English class, and I was helping with her pronunciation."

"Uh-huh," says Joni. "Sure glad it worked out."

The allure of the island draws us too close to the rocky shore where the wind reflects off the cliffs making it impossible to keep the sails trimmed.

"Let's take the sails down and get the fenders out," says the skipper. "We'll motor the rest of the way in."

 ## Provisioning in the Canaries

The tall cliffs on the north side of the island give way to the industrial area of Santa Cruz and eventually to the marina adjacent to the Club Náutico. On the deck of *Toucan*, Shuttleworth and I hold coiled dock lines ready while Captain Ted idles the catamaran close enough to hear the disappointing news.

The dockmaster, in his starched white uniform, sees the boat's name painted on the side and hollers at us, "Hola, *Toucan*." He waves us closer. "We've been expecting you for more than a week."

Captain Ted lifts his arm and replies, "Stormy weather up north. Got caught out in the rain."

I raise my eyebrows and nod in agreement while glancing over at Joni, then to John.

The dockmaster spreads both arms wide in a gesture of helplessness. "Our marina has no room for your catamaran."

He points to a motorized dinghy idling nearby. "We can lead you to another marina to dock."

Captain Ted manages a smile with a half-ass salute. "Okay, *gracias*."

We follow the escort about a mile back up the coast to Dársena Pesquera, an industrial port with a dozen warehouses and tall, heavy-duty cranes ready to load or unload cargo ships. Two cruising monohulls are rafted together behind an oil tanker.

With *Toucan* securely tied to the seawall, Uncle Jim lifts his tired body over the lifelines and steps off the boat with his little old suitcase.

He abandons ship and waits, not so patiently, for a ride into Santa Cruz. Initially, he intended to sail all the way to St. Pete and visit with family, but the storms absolutely changed his mind. More than anyone else, he desires a good night's rest in a real bed, one not in constant motion. He wants a hotel room. Soon.

Within an hour, a compact, four-door sedan arrives, and parks close to where *Toucan* is tied up. A bit too close. Somebody's on a mission that involves us.

A middle-aged man wearing a lightweight sports jacket over a polo shirt climbs out and walks straight toward us smiling and waving his hand. He introduces himself as Clemente, and with broken English offers his services to Uncle Jim and Captain Ted. He wants to be a tour guide, run errands, and answer questions, but he never mentions any fees.

From the cockpit I watch and listen to the stranger. Maybe he works for the man named Fernando, the club member who Ted expects to meet, maybe not. Uncle Jim doesn't care, doesn't hesitate. Right away he asks for a ride and moves his suitcase closer to Clemente's car.

I whisper to John. "What do you make of this guy?"

"He looks legit to me. Let's hitch a ride into town with him."

"Why not? We'll have him outnumbered three to one if he tries to pull anything."

Ted and Joni stay with the boat. John, Uncle Jim, and I hop in the car with Clemente, who acts overly excited and asks too many questions.

I interrupt him. "Clemente, have you had any rain lately?"

He glances in the rear-view mirror. "No rain today."

John re-phrases the question, "How long, no rain?"

"Many days, no rain."

John mumbles, "Must've been nice here for you."

Clemente misunderstands and responds, "Nice to meet you too."

In the backseat, John elbows me in the ribs.

Clemente's friendly personality convinces us that he is sincere in offering his assistance, whether he works for Don Fernando or not. He probably wants to practice his English and show off his hometown at the same time.

Uncle Jim wants a hotel room and I'm sure he'll say something as soon as he can get a word in edgewise.

He does and says, "Clemente, do you know where I can find a medium-priced hotel?"

I should have made a bet with John about how long it would take.

"*Sí señor*, I know a perfect place for you."

He chauffeurs us into Santa Cruz to a quaint hotel two blocks off Plaza de España and parks out front under a jacaranda tree.

Uncle Jim's appearance with his scruffy beard and wrinkled attire, after spending a week at sea in *Toucan's* damp cabin, may raise a few questions. So, I request Clemente's assistance in case the situation needs an explanation. The three of us enter the lobby together and approach the front desk. Clemente takes charge like he owns the place and easily convinces the receptionist to book a room. She completes the registration and hands the key to Uncle Jim with a smile.

Relieved, I carry his suitcase, and we ride the elevator to the second floor. In the room, he kicks off his shoes and sits on the edge of the bed, exhausted. No way he'll ever be shanghaied again.

"Get some good rest. Joni will check on you in the morning."

On my way out, I descend the open staircase to the lobby, grab a book of matches off the front desk, and write the room number on the inside flap for Joni.

In the hustle and bustle of the neighborhood, John takes full advantage of the shady spot as he leans against the back fender of the car, arms folded, and watches while Clemente points down the narrow street giving directions to some restaurant or tourist attraction.

When Clemente takes a breather, I say, "We need to find the Hertz or Avis rental car agency."

"You want a car for better price?" he offers.

We soon make a deal with a local company, thank Clemente for the hot tip, and ask him to stop by the boat in the morning.

In the driver's seat of the rental, while I adjust the rear-view mirror, John says, "I want to get some coins to make a phone call."

Yes, we need to find someone who can fabricate a new rudder, and we'd still like to have another crew member to sail with us across the ocean. It's not a bad deal, especially with all expenses paid, including return airfare.

We drive the four-door Peugeot around town, taking in the sights, and find the main post office. For a token fee, the clerk at the foreign exchange window converts John's British pounds to a bunch of *pesetas*.

"Let's hope somebody answers the phone." John stuffs the paper currency in his wallet but keeps the coins ready. "The man who does the metalwork on our boats was on holiday all last week."

Aha! Another reason why we sailed with only one rudder.

When the international operator announces the cost of making the long-distance connection, John drops *pesetas* into the slots until she says to stop. She then puts the call through to the Isle of Wight. I listen as John explains our predicament and the proposal.

"That went well." He steps out of the booth. "It was Ian Penzon. He's a metalworker and a sailor. We've known each other for years."

"So, how soon can he be here?" I ask.

John replies, "He sounded excited about the sailing offer and said he'll wait for a return call with Ted's approval before booking a flight."

When we tell Ted and Joni about the news, it doesn't take long for them to decide. *Toucan* needs a new rudder and another experienced sailor for the voyage would be helpful. Knowing Shuttleworth, they trust that his referral can satisfy both those requirements.

The unusual opportunity of being invited to sail for weeks on a new catamaran would be hard to pass up, especially for a true sailor.

***

In the morning, Clemente shows up as requested and we take two cars to the airport. Ted rides shotgun with me in the rental and we pick up Uncle Jim on the way. He's flying back to England, and Ian's flight is scheduled to arrive an hour later. John rides with Clemente, who shows us where to park for free. After a grand slam of doors, Clemente says, "I'll wait here and watch the cars."

We split up in the terminal. Ted goes with Uncle Jim to his departure gate. John and I check the flight info board to get Ian's gate number and Ted meets us there a few minutes before Ian shows up.

"There he is," says John when he sees his friend.

Ian has splotches of gray in his beard, a full mustache, and longish, wild hair. He carries himself well—slim and fit. Dressed ready for work, he's wearing faded blue coveralls, slightly oil-stained. He scans the crowd for a familiar face and grins when he sees John.

After introductions, Ted joins up with Ian as we walk to the cars. John and I can't quite hear what they're saying. We don't need to because it looks like Ted is about to put his arm on Ian's shoulder. When John turns my way, I reach out and shake his hand.

***

At the parking lot, Captain Ted instructs Clemente to lead the way to the machine shop he's been telling us about. We enter through an open garage door into a space crammed full of an assortment of rumbling machine tools. The shop manager wipes his hands with an oily rag while Clemente explains that the sailors would like access to his shop for a couple of days. The man eagerly leads us around for a quick tour.

Ted looks pleased and asks Ian, "What do you think?"

"The tools are here," he replies with confidence, and seemingly at ease accepting this crazy assignment. "We need to check his supply of sheet metal and materials before we leave."

The manager, with the captain and Clemente in tow, disappears into the corner office. When they emerge, the manager watches as Ian the metalworker demonstrates his skills on a lathe. His familiarity with the machine tool seals the deal and a quick inventory confirms that the shop has enough sheet metal on hand for fabricating a new rudder.

Returning to the boat, we find Joni relaxing on deck. She has spent the morning reorganizing the galley and making a long list of ingredients she needs from the market. She watches Ian as we approach the boat. How will she react to the rough appearance of a service repairman in coveralls? Let's hope she realizes the value of having another capable Mr. Fix-it onboard while we cross the ocean.

Ted steps close to the boat and introduces Ian from the Isle of Wight.

Toucan's winch farm

Joni waves and says, "Pleased to meet you, Ian. Come aboard and I'll show you around."

"Thank you, ma'am. I'd be delighted." He brushes his hair back as his smile crinkles the corners of his eyes.

Joni flips her hand. "You should call me Joni."

He joins her in the cockpit and Joni pauses because she can see that Ian is admiring the self-tailing winches on the deck, the turning blocks, and the roller furling system for the genoa. She gives him another minute then waves him into the starboard side cabin.

She points forward, "You'll have the v-berth in there, the head is aft of the galley."

"Thanks again. Let me know how I can help."

***

The next morning as we prepare to remove the rudder so Ian can use it as a model while fabricating a new one, Ted asks, "Are you sure we shouldn't rent a crane to lift the boat out of the water?"

Ian says, "It won't be necessary. I checked it out." He adjusts the diver's mask on his forehead. "It's only five feet deep under the boat."

Removing the rudder with the catamaran in the water requires teamwork, in and under the boat. Ted holds the flashlight while John crawls into the aft cabin and waits for Ian to get in position under the hull.

Ian, six feet tall, lowers the mask over his eyes and jumps in. He glances up at me. "Okay, mate, tell 'em to disconnect it."

John unbolts the connecting linkage and Ian catches the rudder while kneeling on the muddy bottom under the boat. He maneuvers it close to the seawall so I can pull it up.

***

While Ian keeps busy in the machine shop, the rest of us cruise around the island. From Santa Cruz, we drive southwest over the mountain on highway TF-5. Ted rides shotgun again. Part way down the other side, he asks me to stop at a scenic overlook. For some reason, his request brings back memories of college days when I had a part-time job driving a taxi at night. We get out for a few minutes to enjoy the Atlantic panorama with a postcard-perfect view of Puerto de la Cruz. Off in the distance to the south, the cone shaped peak of the volcano pierces the sky.

As we continue down to the waterfront, I'm still concerned about Joni's reaction to Ian. "Joni, what do you think of our new crew member?"

She says, "His work clothes caught me off-guard. But so far, he seems like a nice man, very polite."

John speaks up for his friend. "He's an old salt, so you won't have to show him the ropes. Three years ago, when he sailed the Atlantic, they dropped anchor at English Harbour in Antigua."

"That's perfect," says Ted. "We were planning a landfall either in Antigua or the British Virgin Islands."

John continues, "There's two sheltered deepwater harbors on the south side of Antigua."

"That settles it then. We'll sail into English Harbour."

Joni says, "Oh, Ian asked if we have a bosun's chair."

Ted looks delighted as he replies, "What's that mean for us?"

Before Joni can answer, I blurt out, "It means we have another good crew member."

If a halyard gets jammed atop the mast, Ian wants something to sit in while we hoist him up. Makes it safer and easier to work aloft.

The mountain road approaching Puerto de la Cruz passes through a long tunnel, or half of a tunnel because one side remains open for viewing the city's waterfront. There's a boardwalk promenade that overlooks an extensive public swimming pool area and when the wind is out of the west, the ocean spray from waves breaking against the rocks competes with the tall, freshwater fountains in the pools.

We wander into a tourist shop. I spin the rack one more time searching for a postcard that features a fictional, submerged island. I give up and select half a dozen with colorful ocean scenes for family and friends. On the back of the card for Hoff, I print in big letters, "Next stop, Atlantis."

Later, while strolling along the promenade, Joni points and yells. "Look at the lion."

A frisky baby lion seems harmless prancing unleashed from one group of tourists to the next, cute as a toy. Joni asks the man selling ice cream about the lion. He points across the boardwalk to the tall, lanky African twirling an empty leash.

"The man's a loathsome trafficker of exotic felines. He brings the cubs in from Botswana in hopes of turning a handsome profit."

On the way back to the car Joni wonders out loud. "Did he kill the mamma to get the cub?"

Ted shrugs his shoulders. "Probably."

Headed out of town, we follow the main highway south, inland from the coast. The city grows smaller in the rear-view mirror and buildings become sparse. John is in the backseat with Joni and leans forward into the space between the seats.

"While you two were browsing the souvenir shop, I asked around about a place for dinner. The one that sounds best should be farther on up this road."

A few minutes later, we spot a nondescript wooden sign on the side of the road with only one word we recognize—*restaurante*. Ted swivels in his seat to get a better look at the place. When he turns back around, he raises his right hand, like a hitchhiker, giving me the okay to do a U-ey.

The hilltop building looks more like a residence than a restaurant. The gravel driveway leads to a grassy parking area, empty except for a beat-up VW Rabbit close to the back door. Perhaps the place is only open for evening guests. We get out of the car, and I volunteer to go up to the front entrance to scope it out.

A heavyset man wearing a bib apron greets me with a pleasant smile. He looks toward our car, walks halfway down the front steps, and immediately takes charge. *"Hola, amigos."* He waves to the others and invites us in. *"Entra, por favor."*

The show has just begun. Rambling rapidly in Spanish, he leads the way with his right arm outstretched to an empty table big enough for a party of eight in the center of the dining room. Window curtains flutter with the sea breeze and something like the softer side of Santana plays in the background. A young man who bears a striking resemblance to our host moves the extra chairs off to the side. We take our seats. No menus are offered, no questions asked.

A teenage *señorita* wearing a long lacy dress brings place settings followed by two pitchers of sangria with sliced oranges and ice cubes visible through the clear glass. Another young lady carries vases of wildflowers and baskets of bread and fruit to the table. Soon enough, bowls of tossed salads and main dishes arrive, grilled chicken and a casserole of vegetable beef stew, more than we can eat.

Toward the end of dinner, John brings up the subject of *Toucan's* performance. "How many miles did we cover from La Coruña?"

"Yesterday at the marina the log showed a thousand twelve miles but that includes backtracking from the yacht club," I reply. "Roughly, I'd say a thousand nautical miles."

"We left the harbor at La Coruña shortly before noon," says John. "And arrived here in Santa Cruz about the same time six days later, right?"

I take another sip of sangria and scribble on the tablecloth with my index finger. "Six days is a hundred forty-four hours. So, we averaged about seven knots. What would you say our top speed was?"

Ted says, "I saw seventeen point six on the speed-o when we were surfing down the front of a wave."

John grins. "It'll be a while before *Toucan* breaks that record."

The young waitress takes two empty salad bowls from the table.

Joni dabs her lips with a napkin. "This is the best meal we've had in a week. And I didn't have to fix it."

Ted compliments her. "Joni, you took excellent care of us all through the storm. Ain't that right, guys?"

John raises his glass. "Yes, and *muchas gracias*."

When I follow suit and request chocolate covered ice cream bars next time, she tosses her napkin across the table at me. We dine until our bellies are full, then thank our host and his family for the wonderful meal.

The two-lane highway winds its way around the southern end of the island, always with a view of Mount Teide, and leads us back into town where we need to continue provisioning the boat.

An outdoor food market in Santa Cruz, known locally as the African Market, is housed in a complex with a distinctive pink clock tower at the entrance. Hundreds of food vendor stalls and shops arranged around a central courtyard, some decorated with Moorish mosaic tiles, offer the freshest local fruit, vegetables, meat, and dairy products. A variety of nuts, herbs, and spices are imported regularly from West African countries. Strong aromas of spicy foods and burning incense flood the open-air marketplace. Ted loads a bunch of snacks in a canvas sack, chocolate bars and jellybeans, grinning at his haul. I fill several bags with black beans, raw cashews, almonds, walnuts, and Medjool dates from Morocco, enough for weeks, all at bargain prices.

Joni wrinkles her nose and points at the half dozen chickens, freshly gutted, feathers plucked, attracting flies, hanging by their feet from a wire stretched across the booth. She backs away from that stall and moves to the next. With careful planning, she secures enough provisions to feed herself and three hungry sailors for the entire voyage.

John tags along but doesn't need to buy anything. "Sure wish I didn't have to fly back to England."

"We'd love to have you join us for the trip," Ted offers.

Joni agrees. "You and Ian could take turns sleeping in the v-berth on starboard."

"Or we could flip for it." John tries to hide his true feelings. "No, it wouldn't be as exciting with both rudders."

We know he'd love to go with us.

While still in town, we mail the postcards and stop at the airline office just before closing time. John buys a ticket for tomorrow's flight.

Back at the boat, Ian has finished moving his things into the cabin vacated by Uncle Jim and joins the parade to unload the groceries from the car. "Where do you want these canned goods?"

First mate Joni in the galley onboard *Toucan*

"Put everything in the cockpit for now," says Joni. "You guys stay out of the galley. I'll get it organized and put things where I can find 'em later."

While she crams another package into the mini built-in fridge tucked into the rear of the galley, I grab the bag of cashews and hide them under the chart table on the opposite side of the boat. When I straighten up, Ted is watching and smiling.

I turn around and lean against the tabletop directly above my hiding place. "So, where'd you stash your jellybeans?"

Ted goes quickly through the motions of pretending to look high and low for his treats. "What jellybeans?"

Still grinning, he motions toward the steps leading to the cockpit. "Let's bring the wine in from the car before Joni starts complaining about glass bottles."

"I'll be right back."

When I return, Ted is unfolding bath towels in his cabin. I hand him the bottle of volcanic wine from the bodega. "I'd like to save this one for last."

He says, "Definitely, it'll go good with a fresh fish dinner."

We wrap each bottle in clean linens, and he tucks them on either side of the mattresses. For the rest of the day, we keep busy getting the boat shipshape while Joni continues to organize her galley.

***

On the morning of the last full day before departure, Clemente arrives with a note on Club Náutico letterhead addressed to Captain Ted. The cordial invitation from Don Fernando, whose son works with Ted at the pathology lab, offers a poolside buffet for *Toucan's* crew with an apology that he would not be in attendance.

A casual lunch by the pool sure makes sense to me since I tend to avoid the inner sanctum of a yacht club, especially for a meal. The overpriced menus and dress codes don't sit well with real sailors.

However, the barroom is always considered permissible during an awards presentation after a regatta.

Clemente and Ian drive off to the machine shop with the final payment for the manager and return with both rudders, the new one handcrafted by Ian and the one he copied. With the rudders laid side by side next to the seawall, they look alike except for the fresh coat of gray primer on the new one. Ted shows his appreciation with the ol' thumbs up, and Ian grins from ear to ear.

We load both rudders into the inflatable raft. John and Ted climb into the port side aft cabin and wait for Ian to push the rudder shaft up through the housing from under the hull. With Ian standing on the muddy bottom, I lower the new rudder to him, and he holds it under his right arm while feeling for the opening with his left hand. He then raises the rudder shaft high enough for John to bolt it tight to the connecting linkage. The other rudder goes on the same way, just as easy.

Afterwards, as we all stand on the seawall admiring the fine craftmanship, John shakes Ian's hand and declares *Toucan* seaworthy once again.

Ted waves an envelope in the air and starts walking toward the car. "Anybody hungry?"

I catch up to get a closer look at the envelope. The postage stamps from Spain remind me of the guest invitation that Ted received before leaving St. Pete. When I glance over at Joni, she's smiling.

 # The Real Club Náutico de Tenerife

A friendly doorman, not like the one last week, greets us at the front entrance of the yacht club. He reads the invitation from Don Fernando and bows slightly as he opens the door wide.

Back on Florida's Gulf Coast, tucked into protected bays or along the Intracoastal Waterway, we have yacht clubs and sailing squadrons. Socially, there's a big difference. The yacht clubs with their fancy restaurants, swimming pools, and high membership fees cater to the owners and families of the more expensive vessels. The sailing squadrons, which are more relaxed, have a sharper focus on the sport. That is, regattas for many different classes of boats are hosted regularly by the squadrons compared to the one or two held annually at the yacht clubs. The Real Club Náutico de Tenerife falls into the yacht club category.

Arriving poolside, a buxom waitress leads us to a table under a blue canopy. The place is deserted on a Thursday afternoon and obviously the luncheon has been set up as a private affair. The empty Olympic-size pool looks inviting with its calm water but is not the main attraction. The nearby chef's station set up under a matching blue awning against the outside wall of the kitchen captivates our attention.

Delicious aromas of simmering onions and stir-fried seafood with a faint suggestion of garlic lure Joni away from the table. She watches the chef stir his concoction in a large, shallow skillet balanced on four gas burners and returns to the table rubbing her hands together. "We're in for a real treat."

While waiting and lounging around, John asks about my mirrored sunglasses. "Where'd you find those?"

The white plastic frames are not as big as the ones Elton John wore for the cover of his *Greatest Hits* album, but just as memorable. I sit up straight and look over the top of my discount shades.

"Bought 'em in that tourist shop yesterday on the promenade. Super cool, right? She'll never know if I'm peeping at her cleavage. Not that I ever would, not even for an instant." I push the sunglasses back up. "Oh, have you seen the waitress?"

John laughs and glances at Joni as she rolls her eyes, pretending to be embarrassed. Ted turns away in time to notice the man with the tall white hat giving him a nod. He slides his chair away from the table.

"Lunch is ready."

The guys hold back so that Joni, then Ted, can go to the front of the line and fill their plates.

During the meal we all guess at the ingredients and mostly agree that the dish contains a mix of jumbo shrimp, clams, a firm white fish like sea bass, chunks of chicken and chopped smoked sausage. Not andouille, maybe chorizo. Doesn't matter. It's delicious.

The chef, waiting patiently at the buffet, fills my plate a second time, and I return to the table with a big grin. "*Paella*, my new number one menu selection." Ian sits down with his second helping.

Joni says, "You guys better appreciate it. The next meal like this will be served on the other side of the Atlantic."

"We'll make sure it's as good as this one," says Ted.

Stuffed, I pat my belly and turn to Ian. "You ready to take Mr. Shuttleworth to the airport?"

Before we leave, Ted and Joni again extend their invitation to sail with us to Florida. John politely refuses.

At the departure gate, Ian and John shake hands showing as little emotion as possible. Ian says, "See you in a month or so."

John jabs him in the shoulder and reaches for my hand.

I say, "Come sailing with us again and we'll show you some of the Sunshine State."

"I'd love to. You and Ian take good care of *Toucan*."

Boarding pass in hand, John hustles onto the tarmac and joins the sunburned tourists carrying bags of souvenirs toward the plane.

Ian and I, new sailing mates, return to the yacht club to pick up Ted and Joni. Before driving out of town and back to the marina we stop at the maritime customs office to get our passports stamped with exit visas.

Later, restless in my bunk, my thoughts wander. *One more wake-up.* I flash back to an earlier time in Southeast Asia when counting days before a departure date was a serious matter. When you heard somebody brag, "Three days and a wake-up," it meant that on the fourth day, the lucky short-timer would be flying home across the Pacific. Now, about to cross another ocean much differently, I wonder if we have prepared properly.

The water hose bangs against the side of the hull while Ian tops off the tanks. It wakes me up.

Dependable Clemente shows up again knowing the Peugeot has to be returned. Joni asks me to pick up some fresh veggies and a cold six-pack in cans on the way back. When we return, Ted slips a generous gratuity into Clemente's hand, and we bid farewell to our Santa Cruz guide.

The boat is all loaded and ready to go. Ian and I cast off the dock lines and the skipper backs the catamaran away from the seawall with caution, then turns and motors out of the marina.

Joni jumps down into the galley and returns to the cockpit with a bouquet of roses, stems wrapped in paper. "Here we go again."

I glance over at Ian. "The last two times *Toucan* left port the weather turned nasty."

"That's what John told me."

Ted holds up his hand with his fingers crossed. "Maybe this third time's a charm."

Joni pulls some rose petals off and tosses them over the stern as an offering to the wind gods, wishing and hoping for no more stormy weather.

"Where'd you get the roses?"

"At the African Market." She hands me two.

Ian and I climb up on the bench on either side of the captain. Facing aft, we toss a few rose petals and wave. *Adiós amigos,* to no one in particular.

A horn honks in the distance. I believe it's our friend Clemente.

 # Day 1: Say Good-bye to Santa Cruz

Before noon, *Toucan* sails south of Santa Cruz along Tenerife's east coast, two weeks before the summer solstice. With the steep slopes of the volcanic island extending deep below sea level, the captain steers close to shore without fear of shallow water, to enjoy the scenery of the coastal towns advancing up the mountainside.

Feeling good and trying to sound like Billy Joel, I sing to myself and change one of the words to fit the occasion.

Say good-bye to Santa Cruz, say good-bye my baby.

Farther to the south, we have a clear view of the lighthouse at Punta de Abona, a round tower painted white with bands of red and a light at the top that flashes three times every twenty seconds even during the day. Joni snaps a photo and I jump down below for a minute to make a note in the logbook.

Up ahead in the distance, we spot a trimaran sailing in the same direction as us, also on a port tack but farther offshore. I can't quite make out the design or the size, but I can see that they too have their sails trimmed taking advantage of the stiff breeze from the northeast. We're both sailing on a broad reach, but the trimaran is heeled over, making a sizable wake. By comparison, our catamaran sails flat with hardly any heeling or much of a wake.

When Ted changes course to close the gap, I tighten the genoa a bit and lower the starboard daggerboard, anticipating his next move. As we get closer, I identify the trimaran as an older Norman Cross design about the same length as *Toucan* but heavier, and because of the weight difference, it can't compete as far as performance goes.

As we sail past, Joni waves. Ted turns the helm to windward slightly as he looks over his shoulder. I crank the winch to adjust the genoa.

"That won't be the last boat *Toucan* sails over the top of."

"And we have about twice the accommodation of a trimaran of similar size," says Ted.

Pico del Teide grows smaller by the hour as we continue south of Tenerife. The neighboring island of La Gomera comes into view with the historic city of San Sebastián on the east side.

Joni has taken the helm from Ted and the four of us are gazing at the last piece of land we're gonna see for weeks.

I point toward the city. "Columbus made his last stop there before sailing into the unknown."

Ian says, "I know he stopped somewhere in the Canaries."

In 1493 at the beginning of his second crossing, instead of three ships Columbus pulled in with a fleet of seventeen. They needed to make provisions for over a thousand passengers—soldiers, farmers, and, of course, priests to enlighten and convert the natives in the New World.

Ted joins the conversation. "Supposedly, during that second voyage the famous conquistador Juan Ponce de León was onboard."

"Isn't he the explorer who first set foot in Florida?" asks Joni.

"Yes, but not until twenty years later."

Ian asks, "How long did it take 'em to sail across?"

"From what I've read, the first trip took five weeks from here."

"Hey mate," replies Ian, "almost five hundred years later this modern cruising catamaran should make it in half that time."

"Let's hope so," I say. "Supposedly the *Niña* and the *Pinta* had to slow down to stay within sight of the larger flagship, to communicate with Columbus on the *Santa Maria*."

"With what?" asks Joni.

"With lanterns and semaphore flags, maybe cannons if they were far away." After a few seconds, I laugh and joke, "Columbus probably wanted to stay behind so he could turn around if the smaller boats sailed over the edge."

Both Ian and Joni look my way with a smile. In a more serious tone I say, "That story about falling off the edge is not true. Sailors in those days knew the Earth was round."

"That's right," says Ted. "They just didn't know how big it was."

***

Toucan continues sailing to the southwest with the main and genoa on a broad reach toward the dark waters of the Atlantic. The mountain peak on La Gomera blends into the hazy horizon.

Later in the afternoon while Joni steers with a Walkman by her side, Ted asks me to give him a hand in the captain's quarters. He pulls a custom tabletop out from under his bunk. It's heavy and awkward. We maneuver it up into the cockpit and Ian helps attach the front edge to the center cross-section behind the mast. It stands in the middle of the cockpit and needs only one leg for support. The built-in lockers on either side of the table serve as benches wide enough for a party of four and low enough for the boom to swing over our heads.

Joni removes her headphones long enough to say, "It's perfect."

After a few minutes, Ted disappears again into the cabin and returns, this time carrying an unopened cardboard box.

I'm sitting on the bench with my elbows resting on the table and ask, "What's this? Special delivery of gourmet boxed lunches?"

"You wish." Ted replies with a childlike grin. "No, it's an autohelm."

He clears his throat. "With all the stormy weather last time out, we haven't had a chance to use it until today."

Like a gadget freak with a new toy, he empties the box onto the table and doesn't even open the owner's manual. Ted knows about these things. I've never had one on my boat.

"Get the toolbox, and we'll hook it up," he says.

The unit attaches to the top of the rudder shaft on starboard and, with Ted's instructions, I run the electrical cable down to the battery compartment. This portable autohelm can steer the boat in fair weather with no need for a helmsman.

"Okay, once this thing's engaged, let go of the helm," says Ted. "To change course, adjust this dial by hand, and presto, it steers to the new heading."

"But certainly not in rough conditions like last week," I declare.

Ted agrees, "Right, in heavy weather it would be disconnected and stored below."

Ian and I watch as the autohelm steers with minor adjustments left and right to keep the boat on course. We pay close attention for the next hour or so, making sure the new gadget does its job. It does, and we soon learn to appreciate it.

Shortly before sunset Joni shouts from the galley. "Dinner in five minutes."

Ian emerges from his cabin wearing a pseudo dark gray dinner jacket. Actually, it's a lightweight cotton vest fashioned to resemble a dinner jacket. What a hoot! I pull on a clean T-shirt and sit on the bench next to the companionway helping to pass the utensils and chow up from the galley. Ian sits on the opposite side of the table and arranges the plastic plates with their non-skid bottoms. None of us say a word about his jacket vest. I'm not sure if he's joking with us or if he seriously considers it hip, but I kinda like it.

Joni turns off the gas burner and the galley lights, then joins her men in the cockpit with a bottle of Madeira wine. She does a quick double-take at Ian's vest. Ted pops the cork and fills four tumblers with redness.

"*Bon appétit!*"

We enjoy our first fantastic meal on the new table under the boom and watch the Sun as it begins another journey to the bottom of the sea.

***

The warm easterly sea breeze has stayed constant at about twenty knots all day while the autohelm keeps *Toucan* on course. The leading edge of both the mainsail and the genoa slice into the wind to fill the sails and propel the boat to the southwest. The surface of the ocean slowly fades into the darkness. Our water world closes in on us and the sky opens up.

About an hour into our late-night shift, the wind strengthens and the slot between the two sails needs to be opened wider, so the wind can pass through without choking the flow. Ian watches as I tie a line from the clew of the genoa out to a leeward turning block and back to a winch. When I crank the winch to open the slot, the boat speed increases maybe half a knot.

Now it's getting close to the end of our shift.

"Here's a flashlight if you need it." I shut the lid to the bench locker. "I'll turn off the masthead light and the bow lights, so we can see more stars."

"Good idea." Ian places the flashlight at his side. "On this clear, moonless night we'll be able to see the meteor shower better."

That perks me up. "What meteor shower?"

"The lesser known Arietids. They're visible for about five weeks each year starting the last week of May and appear to originate from the constellation Aries."

"How do you know about them?

"An old sailor showed them to me last time I was out here. They're best an hour before dawn but don't expect more than sixty shooting stars per hour."

"All right! Let's keep the lights out until dawn." I love it when it's pitch-dark and no clouds. It reminds me of that line in Neil Young's song: "Blue, blue windows behind the stars."

Toucan's creature comforts include two vinyl-covered bean bag chairs, one red and one blue, filled with thousands of little polystyrene pellets always ready to caress the shape of the occupant. An unwritten rule says that the off-duty crew has first dibs on the bags.

I drag one of the bean bags onto the tramp, fall backwards into it, and wiggle for comfort so that I can gaze in the direction of Aries close to the horizon. Within a minute a bright streak of light flashes across the sky—a shooting star—as the Earth passes through a stream of cosmic debris left by an unknown comet.

From the helm Ian asks, "Did you catch that one?"

"Yeah, but I want more."

He moves to the bench by the table and lowers his voice. "Then you'll have to wait until mid-November for the prolific Leonids."

"Prolific, like abundant?"

"Yes, it varies from year to year, but if the Earth encounters a large outburst from the Leonids, there could be hundreds of shooting stars per hour."

That's exactly what I want right now, a burst of shooting stars to celebrate this feeling I have of being a part of something as large and as joyous as the cosmos. Several minutes pass in silence.

"Hey Ian, does this boat seem small to you?"

"No, definitely not." He sounds quite certain. "When I'm in my cabin it's like being on another boat, plenty of privacy."

"Okay, just checking."

Toucan is perfect for this voyage, but with these shooting stars flashing across the sky, I'm astonished how this boat seems so small floating on this big ocean. I feel small.

Like a morning ritual we witness the predawn shooters for the next few days, enjoying the timeless quality of the night. Then the Arietids join the Sun and the Moon and the constellations in their transit across the sky as routine, commonplace events.

Ordinary? Not for me. I'll never take it for granted again.

"Looking at these stars suddenly dwarfed my own troubles and all the gravities of terrestrial life."

(H. G. Wells, *Time Machine*, 1895)

"Dwell on the beauty of life.
Watch the stars and see yourself running with them."

(Marcus Aurelius, *Meditations*)

Figure 1: Colorized Flammarion engraving, original artist unknown

 ## Day 2: Tropic of Cancer

Originally Ted scheduled shift rotations every four hours starting at midnight, but this morning he made a welcome change. Instead of getting called at four in the morning, the new wake-up call is now loosely scheduled for twilight so both teams can enjoy the sunrise. Sure makes sense since he's the only one who wears a wristwatch. The rest of us have to check the time on the satnav or the wind-up clock in the brass case mounted over the chart table.

Two hours after midnight, every midnight, Ian and I come on watch beneath a gazillion stars until sunrise when Ted and Joni take over. Climbing out of the bunk for four hours in the middle of the night is the toughest part. During the hours of darkness, the shift times are observed, but during the day the shifts overlap. The off-duty team stays on deck, often napping, rather than retreating to the confines of the cabins.

When I stagger out of my bunk about ten in the morning, I read the satnav right away and update *Toucan's* position on the chart. Excited, I spring up into the cockpit and make an official announcement.

"Hey, if anybody's interested, we'll be crossing the Tropic of Cancer soon."

"Why'd they call it that?" Joni asks. "I don't want to get cancer in the tropics."

"I should bloody well hope not," says Ian with his thickest accent.

"Double up on the sunscreen." I know she isn't serious.

From the tramp, Ian looks over his shoulder again. "The Romans named it after the constellation Cancer about two thousand years ago."

Ted says, "It's the most northerly circle of latitude at which the Sun can be directly overhead."

It happens each year on the summer solstice, the day when summer reaches its height, and the Sun shines longest.

Ted takes a sip of tea. "Let us know when we cross over it," and returns his attention to the paperback in his lap, *The Hero with a Thousand Faces* by Joseph Campbell. Joni slips into the galley to conjure up another lunch.

Back at the nav station, I pull out the bag of cashews from my hiding place. The exact position of the Tropic of Cancer varies slightly in a complicated manner over time based on the axial tilt of the planet. Yet the nautical chart shows it at 23.437 degrees north of the equator. *Toucan* is getting close. I can't get another update from the satnav soon enough and even if I could, it wouldn't give our exact position. So, I stash the rest of the nuts and return to the cockpit with a way of celebrating.

"Okay, at the sound of the horn we'll be crossing the Tropic of Cancer. Hold on tight."

Reaching out to the boom to steady myself, I raise the air horn high above my head and point it out to sea. "Three, two, one," and blast it for a second. With a bit of fanfare, *Toucan* sails over the imaginary Tropic of Cancer in broad daylight. I catch a glimpse of Joni in the galley holding a dish cloth in one hand while the other one draws little circles in the air, index finger pointed up.

***

After making my exciting proclamation about the navigational milestone, I duck back down below and turn my attention to the chart. *Toucan* has averaged seven knots during the first night and with the trade winds so steady during June, I make a rough calculation and estimate that the voyage should take us about two weeks, give or take a day or two. Depending on the wind speed, we'll arrive at English Harbour in Antigua with the next full Moon.

Fascination with the satnav is keeping my mind occupied. Since the device needs to receive signals from at least four satellites at a time before it can compute our approximate location, several hours can pass between fixes. Each time it computes a new fix, it overwrites the oldest one because it can only store or remember twenty at a time. I want to save that info for later, so I have been copying the coordinates in a notebook ever since we departed Santa Cruz.

Behaving like the software engineer that I am, I start thinking about a program to read those coordinates from a database and plot *Toucan's* course. The x-axis across the bottom of the sheet will be the longitude and the y-axis the latitude, each set of points represented by a dot or an asterisk.

Coded in FORTRAN, the program will run on the mainframe back at the office and send the plotted data to a tractor-fed line printer on a single sheet of fan-folded green bar in landscape format measuring 15x11 inches. Just for grins.

 ## Day 4: Migrant Swallow

"Oh, the wonder of the great trade-wind! All day we sailed, and all night, and the next day, and the next, day after day, the wind always astern and blowing steadily and strong."

(Jack London, *The Sea-Wolf*, 1904)

Just as predicted, the weather stays perfect with constant winds from the east between ten and thirty knots.

Even though hurricane season has officially begun, the sea remains calm with a light breeze, temperatures in the low eighties. Midafternoon on day four, still under clear skies, *Toucan's* billowing spinnaker pulls our catamaran at a slow pace farther into the Atlantic. With no sail changes needed and the autohelm keeping the boat on course, we lounge around with an eye on the spinnaker as it sways off the bows like one-half of a hot air balloon suspended from atop the mast.

Looking up at it from the tramp, lying on my back in the shadow of the sail, I announce in a loud voice, "This weather is absolutely perfect for sailing."

Ted responds, "They use the word 'prevailing' to describe these trade winds."

"Yeah, like all day and all of the night, for days on end."

Ian puts a bit of a damper on the moment. "One of these days the wind may take a break."

"And it will feel like the thermometer rose really quick," says Ted.

Joni scrambles up into the cockpit like she's seen a ghost ship.

"Something just flew past the galley window."

She looks around and sees a small bird flying in wide circles around the boat. She points at it, turns, and follows it. It's been days since we've seen any birds. We all watch it. Lost from its flock, this migrant swallow has flown too far from shore.

"Ted, look, a messenger from Fesser and Sugar," she says.

Ian asks, "Who are they?"

"Our pet birds back home," she says.

"Ted, do one of your bird whistles. Maybe it'll land on the deck."

Sure enough, when Ted whistles, the bird seems to fly closer. Too exhausted to continue, it lands on deck. Poor thing. Joni rushes to fill a plastic saucer with bread and water, but the birdie won't eat. It hops forward and perches on the lifeline by the tramp, rests for a while, twitters a simple song, poops, then takes off flying in circles again.

Ted whistles and the swallow lands in the same spot. It still won't eat but continues to drop little white puddles. Joni names it Cutie. I tease her and call it Pooper. The little swallow with its tail streamers entertains us all afternoon. It flies in circles, lands to rest with or without whistles, then resumes its graceful flights with long periods of gliding. Did I hear a cheerful warble?

While waiting for dinner, I'm sitting at the table hovering over the companionway within easy reach of the galley. As much as I want to help, Joni insists that the guys stay out of her way. When ready, she passes the goodies up and we arrange the table. Ian and Ted have made a habit of sitting on the other side. Ian wears his "dinner jacket" vest again. Still, nobody says a word about it.

Joni climbs into the cockpit wearing sunglasses and I scoot along the bench to make room. Ted gets up and adjusts the autohelm to change course slightly, so the spinnaker shades the table during dinner.

The bird hops onto the rim of the saucer for a drink then takes off flying again. I squint and turn my head to follow it for a second. "If that little Pooper drops something on my plate, I'll blast the air horn at it."

With her feathers ruffled, Joni whips off her sunglasses. "Oh, yeah? Toot that damn horn and you won't get another plate for days."

"Okay, okay." I raise my hands in surrender and point to Joni's plate. "Never mind little birdie, you can do your business anywhere you want." Ted and Ian stop smiling when Joni looks their way.

At dusk, the lost swallow flies off and never comes back.

***

With the weather cooperating so well, the spinnaker has been up for days. But a little while ago the wind started gusting above thirty-knots. When one of those gusts filled the spinnaker to the point of ripping, the boat happened to be on the front side of a large swell and sped up trying to match the windspeed, making it feel like there was no wind at all. With no apparent wind, the spinnaker floated unfilled and drifted back close to the mast causing the boat to slow down. Seconds later, another strong gust carelessly grabbed the sail and re-filled it with a loud pop. Pow! Yanking the slack sheets taut.

The next gust could blow it out, rip it along one of the seams, and take our only spinnaker out of service. So, we wait for another go-round of the same scenario. This time, when the spinnaker hangs loose, Ian lowers it quickly. We gather the Dacron sail, stuff it in the bag, and drop it in the locker.

We unfurl the genoa, crank it halfway in, and tie it down way out to the port side hull. Then, with only the top hank of the staysail attached, I hoist it while Ian tacks it out to the bow cleat on the starboard hull. We run another line from the clew through a turning block down to a point way forward, so the staysail can be trimmed to feed the genoa.

Toucan sails for hours with this double headsail combination, a modified wing-on-wing, until the wind speed drops below twenty-five knots and stays there for a while. We then lower the staysail, furl the genoa, and hoist the spinnaker again.

At the end of our shift before crawling into my bunk, I make a few calculations at the nav station to compare *Toucan's* performance with Columbus' first voyage. Loaded with provisions and under spinnaker alone, our catamaran sails straight downwind at about a knot faster than half the true wind speed. So, when the wind blows twenty knots, the catamaran averages eleven. That's more than twice the speed of *La Niña*, *La Pinta*, and the *Santa Maria*. I know it isn't a fair comparison boat for boat, but it indicates that the prediction we made at the beginning of the trip will be close.

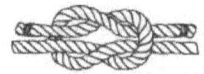 ## Day 6: The Skipjack Tuna

Puffy white clouds like cotton balls hover in the afternoon sky and cast shadows on the surface of the sea. As we sail in and out of the shady spots, the spinnaker shivers in the breeze.

Ted puts down his paperback and stretches his muscles. He checks his wristwatch and glances astern at the boat's wake because the magic feeding hours at dusk are approaching. If we sail too fast, his fishing lure will skip across the surface. Sail too slow and the lure will sink. *Toucan's* speed is exactly right.

Always willing to lend a hand, I remove my headphones and watch as he retrieves his tackle box from the locker under the bench.

"You gonna try your luck?"

Ted rummages through the box. "Yeah, let's see what happens."

He prefers high-test monofilament fishing line and always gives his flashy silver spoon lots of it, so the lure will ride far behind the boat's foamy wake where the curious fish can see it. His fishing pole, when not in use, stays tied to the handholds mounted in the ceiling across from the nav station.

"I'll get your pole."

"Grab a couple pieces of nylon ties while you're down there."

The pole has a proper casting reel, but instead of casting, Ted simply lets enough line pay out and ties the pole horizontally along the rear crossbeam. He reclaims his seat in the bean bag and turns his attention to the next chapter of Campbell's book.

The silver spoon sometimes skips on the surface but mostly stays submerged. Nobody pays much attention to it until hours later when Ian notices a quick jerk on the end of the rod.

"Captain Ted, something big just struck at your lure."

He unties his pole and reels the line in. Both hooks on the spoon are bent straight.

Ted chuckles, "That one got away with a sore lip." He takes the lure off the leader and fastens another one. "Good thing, we never could have landed it in the boat anyway."

Maybe an hour later while Ian takes a nap on the tramp, I'm sitting cross-legged on the bench by the stern mesmerized as I watch *Toucan's* wake, two torrents of bubbles that collide and vanish. All of a sudden, like a jack-in-the-box, a fish on the end of the line jumps up and splashes back into the foam.

"Ted, you've got one on the hook this time!"

He puts his book down and unties the pole again from the crossbeam. "Oh boy!" He smiles and begins to reel the fish in.

I spring to my feet and search the bench lockers for the landing net and the gaff hook.

Ted pulls back on the rod. "It's not puttin' up much of a fight."

Joni grabs her camera and sits at the table ready to capture the action. "Ah, the poor thing's probably tired of fighting."

As the skipper reels the fish closer, it jumps again, and we see its size. The sound of the splash fades away.

Ian has the gaff and holds it ready. "It's a beauty, aye cap'n?"

Ted grits his teeth and reels it in the rest of the way, close to the stern. "Looks like a skipjack tuna."

Ian inserts the gaff into the fish's gill, pulls the nearly dead tuna out of the water, and lands it on the transom deck.

Ted says, "Careful, this is when they often get away." He then bashes it hard on the head a couple of times with a ball-peen hammer to knock it out and retrieves his silver spoon.

He glances over at me. "The Berkley scale is in the locker with the seat cushions."

I grab the scale and attach it to the end of the gaff hook. Ted keeps his hand tight on the tail fin without applying any downward pressure. The needle points to twenty-two pounds.

Joni snaps the shutter on her Instamatic. "You gotta clean it good before it comes into the galley."

Ted prepares the tuna and delivers two sizable fillets ready to cook. Joni turns on the gas burner, opens the window to create a cross breeze, and goes to work. She has about an hour before sunset.

All the guys agree that the best part of each day occurs at dinnertime, no question about it. Every single day Joni prepares a dinner worth waiting for, but when she serves fresh tuna steaks, pan-fried in butter with garlic and chives, we know it couldn't get any better.

The last bottle of wine, the cork goes pop.
Four tumblers filled, didn't spill a drop.
Fricke lifts his up, "Here's to the cook."
Then Joni says, "To the 'jack on the hook."

Ian, Captain Ted, and Fricke holding the scale with the 22 pound tuna.

 # Day 7: The Doldrums

"The goal of life is to make your heartbeat match the beat of the universe, to match your nature with Nature."

(Joseph Campbell, Reflections on the Art of Living)

By the end of the first week, we have sailed halfway across the Atlantic. In another seven days, when the Sun reaches its highest position in the summer sky, we'll arrive at our destination.

The weather has stayed perfect day after day with nothing to relieve the sameness of our days. No more birds. No whales sighted. Definitely no land visible on the endless horizon. Not one drop of rain. Nobody with seasickness or any ailments. No reception from land-based radio stations. No other boats. No board games. Not even a deck of cards or a pair of tumbling dice.

Relaxed, we settle back into bean bag chairs to read paperback novels or listen privately to favorite tunes with headphones plugged into our Walkmans. A wide selection of cassette tapes and extra batteries fill a large Tupperware container. Dozens of paperbacks fit perfectly with their bindings facing up in a separate container, the communal library which is now sorted by genre.

One of the old cassettes is cracked and no longer playable, so I pull the tape out, cut several footlong pieces, and tie them to the shrouds, the standing rigging which holds the mast up from side to side, as high as I can reach. The tapes bounce around, revealing the weakness of the apparent wind while the spinnaker pleads for more.

All morning long the wind has quietly rippled the surface of the sea and now, shortly after noon, the trade winds peter out. One minute, a light breeze barely keeps the spinnaker filled; then the wind dies, the spinnaker deflates, and the telltale tapes hang flaccid from the shrouds.

Ian shuffles forward to the mast and works the halyard winch to lower the sail while I gather it on the tramp. By now we're so well practiced no part of the sail touches the water, a feat not so easy when it's windy. Ian checks the top of the halyard for chafing, then helps stuff the spinnaker in the bag, bottom panels first with the head and the two corners sticking out. That way, it'll be easier to re-connect the halyard and the two trim lines before hoisting it again. Ian holds the hatch cover open while I stash the bag in the locker.

With the trade winds stalled, *Toucan* coasts to a stop, dead in the water. The waves soon settle, and the surface of the sea resembles a sleeping giant's belly, like the ocean is breathing but not quite awake. Widespread, eerie swells make it so spooky and quiet that Ted and Joni come up on deck early.

"What's goin' on?", Joni asks.

Ian and I glance left and right, shrug our shoulders in unison, and turn back to Joni. Nothing is going on. She takes a seat on the bench by the table. Ted lowers himself into the red bean bag chair and looks around like he expects something to happen. Nothing.

For the first time in over a week the boat is adrift, and the trade winds no longer provide a sense of direction. In fact, with the Sun high in the sky, it's hard to tell which way is which. Nothing on the horizon, three hundred and sixty degrees flat. Like the poetic lines from "*The Rime of the Ancient Mariner*," Samuel Taylor Coleridge has written: "As idle as a painted ship upon a painted ocean."

Ian says, "We're nowhere near the doldrums of the Sargasso Sea."

Ted agrees, "Haven't seen any of its brown seaweed on the surface."

Joni looks out across the water. "I wonder how deep it is here?"

"Hold on a minute. I'll see what the chart says."

Toucan's nautical chart from the U.S. Hydrographic Office for the mid-Atlantic explicitly indicates the ocean depth in fathoms.

I return to the cockpit. "At our last fix this morning, the chart says two thousand six hundred and sixty fathoms. And there's six feet per fathom."

Ted does a quick calculation out loud. "If it were only twenty-five hundred times six, that'd be fifteen thousand. So, it's roughly sixteen thousand feet deep."

"That's hard to imagine," says Ian.

Ted helps him out. "Then divide sixteen thousand by fifty-two eighty and you get about three miles deep."

I'm amazed. "We live in a water world."

A few minutes pass and Joni asks me, "Do you remember the last time we were becalmed?" She lifts the hair off the back of her neck.

"I sure do, but it was in shallow water close to land. We suffered in the Florida heat all afternoon."

"Whose boat was it?" asks Ian.

I glance over at him. "We were marooned on my trimaran south of the Marquesas Keys sitting in the cockpit without a whisper of wind, drifting close to the tower at Cosgrove Shoal."

Ted says, "And not enough gas for your outboard to get us twenty miles to Key West." He wipes the sweat from his brow.

To break the monotony during that unpleasant situation, Ted had buried a hook in a doughball, made from a slice of bread, lowered it fifteen feet to the bottom, and caught a gulf flounder for lunch.

"That's when you first impressed me with your talents for catching fish." I wave a hand in front of my face, "Whew! It was hot then and it's getting hotter now. Let's hope the wind picks up soon."

It doesn't, and with the Fahrenheit in the high eighties, it becomes uncomfortably warm. The fireball high in the sky is burning my shoulders and the back of my neck. Flustered with damp armpits and a sweaty crotch, I need to cool off.

"I'm goin' for a dip."

Captain Ted doesn't say anything. Nobody else objects, at least not verbally.

Falling off a boat when it's sailing is never a good idea. Jumping off a sailboat when the sails are down and the wind is dead calm is okay, even in the middle of an ocean. As a competent swimmer, I have no fear of being in the water. It doesn't matter how deep it is so long as I can climb back aboard.

Stepping toward the stern, I squat barefoot on the transom deck five feet above the water and tie a long line to the cleat with a ring buoy attached at the end to prevent it from sinking. I stand tall, fling it overboard, and pause. The Sun's rays shine deep into the water.

Don't know when this chance might come again.

A strange, tranquil feeling sweeps in like an ocean swell, thrilling and vibrant as it pervades my mind. I know from boyhood frolicking that a back flip would be easy but don't want to turn around and face the boat. For this moment, I want some alone time. Can't dive headfirst because my loose-fitting shorts might slip off. So, I jump feet first with toes pointed and both arms tucked tight against my sides. The cool water soothes my suntanned skin as I sink deep.

What a rush!

At the bottom of the plunge, I spread my arms wide, open my eyes, and look up through the clear water. The blurry catamaran appears as two boats.

On the surface I paddle out to the ring buoy and spin around licking the saltwater from my lips. "Come on in, the water's fine."

Ted watches from the cockpit grinning, and Ian is on the tramp pulling his T-shirt up and off. Joni has a towel draped over her shoulders as she yells out to me.

"Yeah, the water looks inviting, but aren't you afraid of sharks?"

The thought hadn't even crossed my mind, and the fact that she mentioned it kind of pisses me off. We haven't seen any shark fins slice the surface all week. Besides, sharks rarely attack swimmers. But her suggestion has power, and I can't shake it loose.

Damn, now I'm spooked. A mini movie plays in my head of an angry shark swiping the calf muscles off one of my dangling legs, then circling back for the other one before the blood draws a crowd.

A casual backstroke gets me to the boat, and I climb over the transom onto the deck. Joni tosses me the towel. While drying off, the rippling network of the Sun's rays penetrates thirty, maybe forty feet deep into the ultramarine, a mere fraction of the way to the invisible bottom.

After Joni goes down into the galley, Ian takes a seat next to me on the bench and says, "I was just about ready to jump in with you."

"You should have. I saw you whip-off your shirt."

He whispers with a smirk, "Did you see any sharks out there?"

"I may have seen a couple small ones circling my legs."

In a few minutes, Ted fires up the engine and when he puts it in gear the telltales on the shrouds flutter back in the slight breeze. Disoriented, he checks the trusty compass to get his bearings and turns the wheel until the needle, with its magnetic magic, points to the "W."

"It feels like we're headed in the wrong direction," says Joni without seeing the compass.

"I'll check the satnav as soon as we get another fix."

Toucan moves westward again not to get anywhere in particular, but to charge the batteries. I take the blue bean bag onto the tramp with my Walkman to drown out the rumbling diesel and avoid its noxious fumes. The phantom sharks swim away searching for mermaids while we sit and wait for Mother Nature.

Later when she freshens the wind from the east, Ted shuts off the engine and we hoist the spinnaker again to harness her power.

 **Day 9: Flying Fish Contest**

"In the dark the old man could feel the morning coming and as he rowed, he heard the trembling sound as flying fish left the water and the hissing that their stiff set wings made as they soared away in the darkness."

(Ernest Hemingway, *The Old Man and the Sea*, 1952)

During the late-night watch, the constellations appear dim and far beyond the half-moon. The trade winds blow steadily as *Toucan* sails into an ocean neighborhood teeming with fish.

Something slaps against the side of the boat.

"What was that?"

Just above the dark water, flashes of hundreds of small fish are fleeing predators, jumping, and swimming in the same direction. Some fly out of the waves flapping their wing-like fins and stay aloft for thirty or forty feet before crashing. Dozens of the aquatic invaders land on the tramp, some in the cockpit.

Suddenly we're wide awake. Ian listens. He knows the sound.

"Flying fish! Let's gather up the big ones and toss 'em in a bucket."

"Right! I'll hold the flashlight, and you grab 'em."

The largest ones measure less than six inches, too small to clean for too little treat. That's the way I think about it but maybe I'll change my mind if we run out of food. So, I search anyway with the flashlight to collect some of the slippery specimens. I grab a few and wonder if

Charles Darwin caught a whiff of flying fish as they thrashed about on the deck of the HMS *Beagle* a hundred and fifty years ago.

Ian drops two more in the bucket.

I toss mine in and say, "Maybe we should put the lid on."

"They can't fly out without a running start."

"You mean a swimming start."

The Englishman, with his different sense of humor, presents a crooked smile and pinches his nostrils. Flying fish stink.

***

The barrage lasts only a few minutes while the catamaran cruises through the neighborhood frenzy. The "fishermen" count their catch and wait for the shift change so they can boast about the ones that didn't get away.

The newsworthy event of the bizarre activity on *Toucan* will certainly be splashed across the front-page morning edition of the *Atlantis Tribune*, or so I imagine, in large bold type letters. But Ted and Joni don't need to read it in the newspaper. After arriving on deck at sunrise, they hear all about it within minutes from two eyewitness reporters who provide all the exciting details before retiring to their cabins, proud of their haul.

Four hours later, when Ian and I come back on deck, we discover that Ted and Joni have also encountered a school of the strange fliers and collected the unlucky ones in a separate bucket.

And now the game begins with Ian and me off to a good start.

We designate Ted and Joni as the home team and for the next two nights, our international team maintains the lead. Up until this point, the average fish measured three inches, none smaller than about two inches.

But then, dammit, during the last shift of the game the home team collects dozens of tiny flying fish, more like millimeter fishlets, which increases their score far into the lead.

Joni picks up their container and places it on the bench next to the table so Ian and I can get a good look.

I reach in and scoop up a handful. "These little ones don't count."

Teammate Ian plays with his beard and nods in agreement.

"They do so," demands Ted, pretending he's serious.

The little fishies tremble from my hand back into the bucket.

"You're changing the sizing rules after the fact."

"What rules?" says Joni, hand on her hip, jerking our chain.

***

Later, the international team lodges a protest with the office of Poseidon but grows tired waiting for a reply. The game ends when we can't decide how to count the fishlets and both teams claim themselves as winners.

During dinner for the next few days, I drop subtle hints referring to our team's catch with large adjectives and theirs with smaller ones.

"Yeah, but our bucket of big ones would've outweighed all your little fishlets."

The joking and the novelty soon wear off. Fish flying into the cockpit and onto the tramp becomes a routine nuisance. Ian still collects the large ones, though, and hangs them by the tail from the lifelines to dry. He claims their nutritional value, like brisling sardines, could keep a man from starving to death.

 ## Day 10: Visitors

Like yesterday and the day before, the mainsail stays down and tied to the boom while the spinnaker alone pulls our catamaran closer to the West Indies. We're sailing on a lonely seascape and have had no contact with any other member of the entire human race since leaving the Canaries. After not seeing another vessel for ten days, we have become relaxed and less vigilant.

Shortly after lunch, the autohelm starts making a scraping noise every so often but continues to steer a straight course.

Standing in the cockpit facing aft, I hold onto the boom and sweep my other arm through the air. "It's so beautiful, the vastness. Where is everybody?"

"They're sleeping. Want me to wake 'em"?

Ian plays with his beard and laughs at his own wisecrack. By now the two of us have grown accustomed to the easy-going banter. As you can imagine, it gets monotonous out here with no escape.

There's the slight sound of a splash, then another, closer.

"Look!"

Spotted dolphins, perhaps a dozen in the pod. They ride the bow waves and swim between the hulls.

Since the trampoline provides the best place for viewing, we scramble forward and pass by Ian's flying fish hanging from the lifelines. We lie flat on our bellies with the crossbeam under our armpits and reach down into the saltwater spray to almost touch the playful visitors.

A gregarious bunch, they break the surface and seem to enjoy eye contact with the alien creatures on the strange boat with two hulls. I'd sure like to change places with one of them only for a few minutes.

Too soon the curious dolphins swim away. I get up and balance myself at the base of the mast to watch but lose sight of the fast swimmers. Maybe they'll come back later for a second look.

***

Near the end of the mid-day shift, I scan the horizon again and with the Sun high in the sky, visibility at all points of the compass can't get any better. I do a double-take, squint, and without a doubt see a large white ship approaching from the west. Aha! More visitors. We're no longer alone in this water world. I raise the binoculars and watch for a few minutes. *Toucan* and the oncoming vessel will not collide so long as we both maintain our headings.

I step down into the cockpit and pass the binoculars to Ted. "There's a container ship on the western horizon about ten miles out."

He rotates the focus dial to suit his liking and watches the approaching ship. "They'll pass us to the south but let's keep a sharp lookout." He returns the binocs.

"Will do. I wonder where they're going?"

Ian stands up and looks. "West Africa would be my guess." After a short pause, he says, "I read recently that the number of container ships worldwide has more than doubled in the last ten years."

"There's gonna be a lot more." I refocus the glasses. "And they probably drop a shitload of containers when the seas get rough."

Ted checks to make sure Joni is busy down in the galley and lowers his voice. "It's true. Thousands of containers fall off every year, most often during storms. Some float on the surface for days before filling with water and sinking."

"That's scary. It would be like sailing into a steel box, big as a car." I glare at the oncoming vessel. "Or worse, crashing into one during a late-night storm."

Ted steers the conversation away from dire straits. "Go ahead. Try to make radio contact."

Jumping down into the cabin, I grab the microphone and stretch the coiled cord to its full length. On the top step in the companionway, staring in the direction of the large ship—like it matters—I make the call using my radio operator's voice, which has a serious tone.

"*BigWhiteContainerShip, BigWhiteContainerShip*, this is sailing vessel *Toucan*. Over."

Joni climbs out of the galley, sits at the table, and waits. I return to the nav station, make an entry in the logbook at 1:32 p.m., and adjust the volume knob on the radio all the way up.

We sit in the cockpit and wait … and wait.

Ian steps up to the base of the mast and eyeballs the ship. "I bet the radio officer on the bridge wants to get permission from the captain before responding."

"Yeah, and he's probably napping in his private quarters."

Joni rubs her fingers in circles on her temples. "Maybe if we all sit and stare at it, they'll pick up on our vibes."

Ted speaks with a stern voice. "When they respond—if they respond—ask if *Toucan* shows up on their radar screen."

Large vessels equipped with radar systems can detect each other even in a dense fog at night. But sadly, sailboats may never show up on a radar screen because of their smaller size and lack of metal in the framework.

Ted wants to know if *Toucan* shows up with its aluminum mast standing fifty-six feet tall. We have all heard the story about the container ship that collided with a sailboat and didn't notice until after arriving at port with the boat's mast dangling from the bow.

After what seems like hours, a drowsy masculine voice comes back with a heavy European accent.

"*Toucan*, this is *BigWhiteContainerShip. S*witch to Channel 68. Over."

All right! This is bigger than front page news. Racing into the cabin, I nearly trip and fall but quickly switch from Channel 16 to 68.

"*BigWhiteContainerShip,* this is *Toucan.* We're about eight miles off your port bow and would like to know if you can see us on your radar screen. Over."

"Stand by *Toucan*. Over."

All four of us sit in the cockpit and wait. What is taking so long? Ian is comical with his hands in his lap, twiddling his thumbs.

The spinnaker drifts left and right obstructing our view of the big ship, so Ted tweaks the autohelm to change course slightly and Ian trims the sail to the new heading. After another couple minutes, the distant voice comes back over the airways.

"*Toucan*, this is *BigWhiteContainerShip*. Over."

Ted looks my way and nods, so I press the talk button.

"This is *Toucan*. Go ahead."

"We can see your catamaran with its colorful spinnaker even without binoculars, but your vessel does not show up on our radar screen. Over."

Ted shakes his head in disbelief. "Ask him where he's headed."

"Okay, thanks. That's good to know." I glance again at the ship. "By the way, we're headed for Antigua. What's your destination? Over."

The accented voice responds immediately. "We departed from Montreal last week and we'll dock in Lagos for three days then on to Cape Town." He pauses until the static interference clears. "When you drop anchor in English Harbour, be sure to talk to Duncan at the chandlery for info on the best restaurants. Over."

Joni jumps up, spins around, and does a little dance step.

I respond with, "Okay, roger that, and thanks for the tip. Over."

"And may the trade winds stay strong at *Toucan's* back. Switching to Channel 16. Over and out."

Two clicks of the transmit button acknowledge his final adieu and with the mic in its clip on the side of the radio, I switch back to the hailing frequency.

Joni does another dance step, this time with both arms raised.

"Say hello to Duncan, say hello to Nelson."

Ian and Ted bust out laughing and that gets me started.

The big white ship with all its containers disappears gradually beyond the eastern horizon. At the nav station I make another entry in the logbook at 2:26 p.m. and note that the ship has come and gone in less than an hour. Reaching under the chart table into my private stash, I grab a fistful of cashews and climb into the cockpit.

Ian sneaks off to his cabin for some shuteye and Joni returns to the galley. Ted has officially started his watch, so I shuffle forward to the tramp to take a nap in the shade of the spinnaker, hoping to hear the blowhole chuffs again if the dolphins return.

***

At dinner, with the day's activities fresh in our minds, Ted asks me, "How long was that ship in view today?"

"Not even an hour."

"So, for about half an hour, it was past us and going away."

I know where this conversation is headed and look at Ian for support.

He says, "If we're ever on a collision course, we'll have less than thirty minutes to make a correction."

"That's right, guys," says Ted. "Their radar wouldn't see us, and the ship would hold its course. We need to stay alert, no napping on duty."

"Definitely not." I point to the autohelm, "That blind device would steer us straight into a collision."

"Crashing into the steel hull of a container ship would destroy *Toucan*," says Joni. "We'd be sunk and treading water."

"Shark bait is what we'd be," says Ian.

 ## Day 12: Late-Night Flashback

A warm tropical breeze fills the spinnaker, colorful panels of Dacron swaying in the light of the Moon, dragging us westward at a comfortable clip. If we could pick up a radio station, the weather forecast would be the same as yesterday and days before: "Clear skies with a steady breeze from the east, Fahrenheit in the low eighties." Perfect conditions for sailing straight downwind with only one sail hoisted. The mainsail is still undercover resting on the boom, the genoa is furled tight, and the amazing autohelm continues to steer as it has since day one.

Ted and Joni are sound asleep in their cabin while Ian and I struggle to stay alert here in the cockpit. It's so peaceful during the early morning shift between 2 a.m. and sunrise that it becomes positively boring. Last night and the night before we both fell asleep for a while but not at the same time.

Moonlight in the cockpit is bright enough to see without a flashlight and that's the way we like it. We're watching the Little Dipper with the North Star in its handle, an easy way to verify that the autohelm is keeping us on course.

Ian relaxes on the bench along the back of the cockpit next to the helm, and I'm sitting at the table within easy reach of the winches. In another hour we'll hit the bunks and be fast asleep within minutes.

Wait a second. It looks like Ian is nodding out already.

"Hey, you awake?"

"Now I am." He lifts his head and scratches his beard. "I was resting my eyes. What day is it?"

I know from the logbook. "It's the eighteenth of June."

"I mean, what day of the week is it?"

"Oh, I'm not sure. Why?"

Ian glances up at the spinnaker. "I was just sittin' here thinkin' about how weird it is not knowing what day it is."

"There's probably a calendar in the cabin."

"Forget it. I really don't care. I'm just looking forward to the day when we see land again."

"It'll be on the day when the Moon is full."

"Should we call that Moon-day or Land-day?"

"Go back to sleep."

I move forward to the base of the mast, the best place to scan the full horizon. Shimmering moonlight casts silver reflections off the dark water while *Toucan* sails alone. We need to stay awake and alert. I really don't want Ian to fall asleep, so I'll keep talking. Tell a joke or something.

"Hey, wake up. One of the rudders fell off."

Ian raises his head again and responds well to the joke. "Couldn't have been the one I built."

The good retort makes me smile. "That's right. The one you built is still holding on."

Now that I have his attention, I say, "Sure could have used your expertise a couple of years ago."

"When you lost a rudder?"

"No, worse than that."

I always enjoy telling this story.

"My boat was anchored in a shallow bay on the south side of St. Pete, apartment complexes and condominium towers in all directions. I took the day off work to do some maintenance."

"That never ends." Ian sits up and rubs his eyes. "What kind of boat do you have?"

"A trimaran, a Newick Native design."

"That's a classic," says Ian. "What happened?"

"It was a quiet Tuesday morning until I heard a van drive up towing a trailer. Two guys got out and unloaded a Jet Ski into the knee-deep water. The tallest guy straddled the water scooter, raised the handlebar up off the seat, and started the engine."

"How far away were they?"

"Couple hundred yards, or meters to you. After the first guy took off, the other dude at the shore watched and waited for his turn. When they switched drivers, they kept the engine running and were careful not to let go of the handlebar, like something was wrong with the throttle."

I raise my right hand and twist an imaginary handle. "As predicted, after a couple of go-rounds, the Jet Ski got away from them and raced out into the bay, stuck on full-throttle, handlebar folded down, rooster tail flying high."

"Oh, no," says Ian.

"Those things are designed to idle when a rider falls off, and turn in a tight circle, so the rider can climb back on. Not this time. It raced at full speed, out of control, and made wide circles in the bay. Nobody was gonna climb back on this one."

I get up and turn toward Ian. "Both guys at the shoreline stood with their mouths open like this." I place my palms against the sides of my head and pantomime a scream.

"Don't tell me it rammed your boat."

"I kid you not. I climbed out of the cockpit and watched the damned thing as it made one complete circle around my boat."

Extending my arm, I spin around slowly while pointing at the imaginary Jet Ski. "When it got upwind fifty yards off the bow, it made a sharp turn as if on remote control and headed straight for my boat."

"You must have been freakin' out."

"Yeah, a little. It was like watching a scene in one of those stupid Hollywood flicks, unbelievable. At top speed, the Jet Ski glanced off the starboard side of the main hull and left a two-foot gash just above the waterline."

Exaggerating a bit like fishermen do, I hold my hands out about three feet apart and shake them. "Now I was freakin' out. It kept going, turned again, raced half a mile across the bay, slammed into a concrete seawall, and sank."

Ian lets out a hardy laugh. "A fitting end."

"That's what I thought too. I jumped in the dinghy and headed for shore. Got their names and the license plate numbers for the police report."

"Somebody needed to pay for the damage," says Ian.

Deflated, I sit back down on the bench. "As it turned out, the two guys were exchange students from Switzerland and staying in a house they had rented from the Jet Ski owner who was in jail in Tampa."

"That takes the cake," says Ian. "Back up a minute. How much water was leaking into your boat?"

"I paddled back out to check. Luckily, not much. The damage was above the waterline, so I stuffed some old rags in the gash and duct taped it on both sides until I could get the boat hauled out."

"Did you call the police?"

"Yeah, when I got back home. The St. Pete police department said it was out of their jurisdiction since it happened in Boca Ciega Bay. Big help they were. I called the Coast Guard, and the trooper said something about calling the Marine Patrol. I hung up on him. Guess who had to foot the bill."

"Don't need to guess," says Ian.

I crank the starboard winch a couple of turns and continue telling the story. "The following weekend, I had to motor the boat with that temporary patch twenty miles to the boatyard."

"Who did the repair job?"

"Pete, he's a boat builder and a member of our sailing club."

"Oh, the joy of boat ownership," says Ian, watching the spinnaker.

"You got it." I tap my knuckles on the tabletop. "Imagine the cost of *Toucan* so far."

Dawn approaches, and the wind shifts enough to cause the spinnaker to flutter, so Ian lets the trim line out a little on the port side. Ted and Joni climb into the cockpit and join us for the morning show. Once again, the rising Sun slowly illuminates an exquisite, silent seascape.

Day 13: Sextant vs SatNav

"Captain Nemo, by the help of his sextant, took the altitude of the sun, which ought also to give the latitude. He waited for some moments till its disc touched the horizon. Whilst taking observations not a muscle moved, the instrument could not have been more motionless in a hand of marble."

(Jules Verne, *Twenty Thousand Leagues Under the Seas*, 1870)

After dinner as the Sun approaches the horizon, Ted goes to his cabin and returns with an old hardwood box, worn on the edges. He opens the hinged top and extracts a polished brass sextant. He fiddles with it on the table, inspecting the mirrors. Sliding the index bar back and forth, he stops it at about forty degrees. It looks to me like he's checking the alignment.

Meanwhile, Ian is relaxing in the blue bean bag chair on the tramp. When Ted clears his throat, Ian turns and sees the sextant. He works his way back to the cockpit and joins Ted at the table.

"That's a fine-looking instrument," says Ian. "Why'd you wait so long to bring it out?"

"We haven't needed it." Ted glances at Ian. "But if we get caught in the doldrums again like last week and run out of fuel keeping the batteries charged, it will come in handy."

Ian gives Ted a look of approval. "Yep, it's a practical backup for the satnav."

"It's here if we need it," says Ted.

After a few minutes, the edge of the spinnaker starts to flutter so I crank the starboard side winch half a turn to trim it and tweak the autohelm to change our course farther south of west.

As far as I know, nobody in our sailing club carries a sextant on their boat these days. I've never used one. It's like a long-lost art.

"Hey Ted, when did you learn to use a sextant?"

"Joni and I took a course in celestial navigation this past winter in St. Pete at the Coast Guard station."

"Cool. Let's test it. Take a couple of sights to find our location."

Joni hollers up from the galley. "I'll tell you guys where we're at. We're in the middle of the frickin' ocean."

Ted raises his eyebrows. "She's right."

He then turns his attention back to the brass instrument. "What would you like to test, the sextant or my ability to use it?" he says with a grin.

"Both." I nod toward the sextant. "I'm curious about its accuracy."

"Yeah, so am I," says Ian.

"Well, don't expect too many digits to the right of the decimal point," says Ted. "This evening I'll take a reading with Polaris to get our approximate latitude. That's the easy one. Then tomorrow before lunch,

I'll get several readings with the Sun to determine local noon and calculate our longitude using the time on *Toucan's* clock."

Ian asks, "Do you have a copy of the Nautical Almanac?"

"Yes, it's down there on the shelf," says Ted. "And just so you know, before setting sail from England we synchronized *Toucan's* clock and my wristwatch to Greenwich Mean Time and haven't changed them since."

After sunset, Joni disappears into her cabin. On the horizon, the line between sea-green and sky-blue slowly blurs to gray. When darkness sets in, Ted takes the sextant over to the starboard side of the cockpit and fixes his sights on Polaris or some bright star nearby. I go down to the nav station, flick on the light, and make a note of our latitude location from the latest satnav fix about twenty minutes ago.

Returning to the cockpit I ask Ted, "What did you mean when you said getting our latitude with Polaris was easy?"

"Since it lies nearly in a direct line with the axis of the Earth's rotation above the North Pole, its angle above a ship's horizon is approximately the same as its latitude." He writes something in his notepad. "Navigators in the northern hemisphere have been sailing the oceans forever with Polaris as their guide."

I suddenly realize we won't be able to fairly compare the satnav reading with the sextant measurement. The two readings will be out-of-sync, taken at different times. The satnav only computes our location after it receives signals from at least four satellites at the same time. So, our latest fix happened maybe an hour or so prior to Ted's measurement with the sextant.

Ted returns to the table with the sextant dials locked, moves the portable lamp closer, and underlines the angular measurement in his notepad.

"Look at that." I compare his with mine. "The numbers are only slightly different."

Ted looks up from the notepad. "They're close enough."

"So, the ancient mariners knew their approximate latitude from the stars, but how did they know the longitude?"

"They didn't," replies Ted. "The problem of determining longitude wasn't solved until the mid-1700s by an Englishman named John Harrison."

"Are you telling me that Vasco da Gama, Magellan, Columbus, and the rest of 'em never knew how to determine their longitude?"

"That's correct."

Back then the seafarers navigated by dead reckoning and guessed at their position of longitude. Solving that navigational problem became such a major quest in the 1700s that kings and queens in Europe offered sizeable prizes for a solution. It became known as the Longitude Problem.

"Why couldn't they estimate their location based on how long they had traveled?"

"Clocks in those days weren't accurate enough until Harrison invented the chronometer in 1730," says Ted.

"Just having an accurate timepiece onboard wouldn't have allowed them to figure out their longitude?"

"Not at all, it wasn't that simple. They needed to determine local noon by measuring the maximum angle of the Sun with a sextant, then refer to pre-calculated tables in an almanac to get the longitude."

"What about your wristwatch? Is it accurate enough?"

"Yes, it's a late-model Seiko," says Ted. "It's probably more accurate than the ship's clock. We should compare one against the other."

"What time do you have now?"

Ted glances at his watch. "In about ten seconds, it will be 9:56."

"Just in time for another beautiful night under the stars in the middle of nowhere." I lean into the companionway and check the time on *Toucan's* clock. The minute hand still vibrates after jumping to 9:56. It's time for a shift change.

Joni climbs into the cockpit and sees us at the table with the sextant and the notepad. She moves across without stopping and steps down into the galley to start the water boiling for coffee. Then I hear her say, "I already told you guys where we're at." Minutes later she hands Ted a hot mug of coffee and sits at the table.

Before heading for my bunk, I ask Ted, "Are you gonna take readings tomorrow with the Sun?"

He takes a sip and turns off the lamp. "Might as well; it'll be a fun exercise to see if the longitude calculation also comes close to the satnav reading. So, we'll want the readings to be accurate to the second."

***

The next day, half an hour before noon, Ted positions himself with the sextant and every five minutes makes a note of the Sun's angle above the horizon. He needs to know when the Sun reaches its highest point in the sky, which defines local noon regardless of the time on the clocks.

After an hour or so, he joins me at the table in the cockpit and places the sextant in the box next to the notepad. "Now I'll need the almanac to figure out our longitude."

Joni calls up from the galley. "Clear the table. Lunch in five minutes."

We obey her request at once. Right away. That's what good sailors do when somebody goes to all the trouble of fixing a meal. Joni treated us to the last of the skipjack tuna yesterday but knows we'll be grateful, no matter what she cooks up. Fresh fruit and veggies disappeared from the menu days ago, so she gets creative with canned goods.

After lunch, I retrieve the nautical almanac and set it in front of Ted. He quickly finds the correct reference table and finishes calculating the longitude which he writes at the bottom of the page. He spins the notepad around to face me.

I say, "So, this is how far west you think we were before lunch?"

"Yes, approximately," says Ted with confidence.

"Okay, now we need to add to that your estimate of how far we've gone since then, based on our current speed." I spin around and head for the companionway. "I'll do the same with the latest satnav fix."

Ten minutes later, we meet back at the table with two estimates of *Toucan's* approximate longitude for comparison. The readings are close, certainly close enough to find Antigua in the Caribbean. Of course, in the middle of Joni's frickin' ocean, it doesn't really matter so long as we keep sailing toward the sunset side of the Atlantic.

We know we're being boys with toys, but it feels good knowing we have a dependable and accurate backup to the satnav.

Like Ted says: "It's here if we need it."

Ever since departing the Canaries we have enjoyed watching the Sun, the Moon, and the stars moving across the sky. There isn't much else to watch. The number of hours between sunrise and sunset has stayed consistent for the entire crossing with about thirteen hours of sunlight every day.

The waxing Moon rises and sets on its own schedule and has sparked a guessing game about the exact time it will pop up. Two days after leaving Santa Cruz, it appeared as a crescent: a week later, as a half. Now, after fifteen days, the full Moon rises on the evening of the summer solstice, right after sunset.

At the end of the evening shift while reclining in my bunk with the Walkman, I listen to Jagger and Taylor jam with "Moonlight Mile," the first minute or so anyway, and fall asleep for a few hours.

Back on deck later, the brightest night of the voyage continues with some serious moonlight. Shortly before dawn, the Moon approaches the horizon directly ahead off *Toucan's* bows. And, minutes later, the Sun will rise off the stern, making both globes visible for a short time on opposite horizons. One spectacular scene is about to happen without a cloud in the sky.

Rocket scientists and astronomers often lecture about the alignment of solar system objects similar to this one. They use the word syzygy but I'm not sure of the spelling or the pronunciation. It's probably from Ancient Greece.

Ten minutes before the shift change, before sunrise, I bang on the cabin top to wake up the home team. For fun, Ian and I devised a little stand-up comedy routine to share and to celebrate the summer solstice. Standing side by side in the cockpit facing south, I extend my right arm and point to the setting Moon. Ian points his left arm at the rising Sun.

When Ted and Joni arrive to begin their morning shift, it takes them a while to figure out what the early-morning clowns are doing. We're in sync. Ian raises his outstretched arm and I lower mine.

"You two are getting crazier by the day." Joni shifts her eyes to the sunrise, then to the full Moon setting in the west.

Ted lowers himself to the bench and stares with a sense of awe.

"A beautiful sight, especially out here with such clear skies and an unobstructed view."

We enjoy the show for only a few minutes as the two orbs dance together on opposite horizons. We look to the west, then east, then back to the west.

When the Moon sets, the performance ends, and I move over to the companionway ready to crash, stage left. It's easier now to understand why early civilizations considered themselves at the center of the universe.

***

After another four-hour nap, I check the satnav and make a note in the logbook about how the latest fix, an hour ago, showed our position to be within twenty miles of Antigua.

On deck, the Sun is burning the back of my neck as I sit in front of the starboard daggerboard resting my elbows on my knees, holding the binoculars focused on the western horizon. There, right on schedule though barely visible, a faint mountaintop appears. Now it's gone. Now it's back. I lower the glasses and shade my eyes. Squint. Is that the top of a mountain?

Throughout history sailors have reported seeing mirages at sea, off in the distance hovering just above the horizon. Sometimes the image resembles an island, a distant shore, or often another vessel.

The Italians refer to the image as a *Fata Morgana* because they once believed that the Arthurian sorceress Morgan the Fairy, a powerful enchantress, with her witchcraft would conjure up images of false land to lure sailors to their deaths.

What I see is no *Fata Morgana*. We have finally arrived.

 ## Day 16: Land Ho!

"I thought you understood," he said. "The world is your teacher. It will be all around you. The ocean and the wind and the stars and the moon will all teach you many things. The wind is blowing, adore the wind."

Pythagoras, The Symbols, "Symbol 8"

None of the others have seen it yet. Ted turns another page, still deeply involved with Campbell's book. He must be getting close to the end. Ian's on the tramp in a bean bag chair splicing the heavy-duty nylon anchor rode to the chain. Joni is down in the galley. She said something earlier about adding canned pineapple slices in a heavy syrup to a fruit salad.

I should probably wait another hour or so before making an announcement but the neurons in my brain are firing in all directions. Where's that Lombard cannon or, better yet, a cherry bomb firecracker when you need it? I visit the satnav twice more and pace back and forth on deck trying to keep from staring at the mountaintop, but all the while the young boy in my head is jumping and cheering. Not able to wait any longer, I climb up on the boom, point, and shout, "Land ho!"

Nobody has to ask which way to look. As expected, it's right there, straight ahead. A large green mound of Mother Earth rising above sea level. Strangest damn thing we've seen in weeks. Strange, beautiful.

Ted bookmarks his page and gets up. "If that's not Antigua, we're stopping anyway."

Ian climbs out of the bean bag with a snap shackle in his hand. "I'll be able to tell for sure when we get closer." He turns toward Ted. "The entrance to English Harbour is on the south side of the island."

With its deepwater anchorage, naturally well-suited to protect ships from hurricanes, English Harbour became a base of operations for the British Royal Navy during the eighteenth century. Antigua and Barbuda, the neighboring island to the north, eventually joined the British Commonwealth as an independent state, with Queen Elizabeth II as the reigning monarch.

Ted rubs his chin and looks at Ian. "What if the anchorage is too crowded?"

"Our second option will be Falmouth Harbour which is larger and also on the south side," says Ian, remembering from his last visit.

Joni puts her two cents in. "I'm with the captain. Let's pull in no matter what. You guys can buy me lunch, dinner, and breakfast. *Toucan's* galley is now officially closed." She points forward to the lifelines. "And Ian, you can toss those dried flying fish overboard."

The azure sky above the open ocean remains clear, but as we sail closer, puffy clouds become visible hovering over the island. The cliffs along the southeast coast, facing the constant brunt of the trade winds, are small compared to Tenerife.

From our point of view, the island with its rocky seashore appears to be undeveloped like a paradise. No resorts or even buildings are visible. The cities and towns must be tucked away, protected from the wind and the waves. A motor yacht bounces through the choppy water and the lone helmsman waves, probably on his way to a fish haven. Squawking seagulls ignore us and follow him.

After climbing down from the boom, I move onto the bench to disengage the autohelm. The cylinder feels warm to my touch.

"Ted, it feels like the autohelm has overheated."

The skipper takes the helm. "The manual said it was maintenance-free, but I guess the bearings could use a drop of oil."

The autohelm has performed like a champ all the way across, Santa Cruz de Tenerife to Antigua in sixteen days.

Ian helps me bring down the spinnaker for the last time, and we slip it in the sail locker. He looks toward the harbor. "Let's get the anchor ready, mate."

In La Coruña the boat stayed tied to the docks and in Santa Cruz to the seawall, so the anchor has been stored in the locker since leaving England.

I lift the hatch cover to the anchor locker. "This thing is brand-new and has been patiently waiting for its first assignment."

Ian looks around and returns the humor. "What a great place to start a career in anchoring."

He then hauls the anchor out of the locker, connects it to the chain with a large stainless shackle, and spreads the nylon line out on the tramp ready for deployment.

As we get closer, the shallow water by the shore appears crystal blue. Trees, beautiful green trees, come into focus. Off to starboard a red navigational bell buoy rocks in the waves and sounds so sweet, tolling for *Toucan*. As we motor into the harbor, we must look like a bunch of wide-eyed kids when they arrive at the carnival for the first time.

Lush green foliage surrounds the area. Bougainvillea and wild plumbago shrubs with their white flowers dot the hillsides. Along the beach, one-story houses are flanked by tall palm trees bending with the breeze.

"I'm so glad we didn't arrive at night," says Ted.

Half a dozen monohull sailboats have dropped their anchors in the middle of the harbor, so we find a spot in shallow water close to the beach. Joni sits at the table and listens to the sound of chain links clanking as Ian lowers the hook until it hits bottom. Ted backs the catamaran away to snug it up, then shuts off the engine.

Ian rubs his hands together, picks up the airhorn, and blasts it out toward the ocean. "On behalf of the Queen, welcome to the Commonwealth." He pauses. "And to Captain Ted and first mate Joni, congratulations on a successful crossing."

Ted salutes. "Thanks, Ian. We should all be grateful nobody was injured out there." Joni nods in agreement.

Horns toot on some of the other boats. Two bikini-clad teenage windsurfers sail close astern and wave. A dark-feathered cormorant struggles out of the water with wet wings flapping furiously during take-off. The aquatic bird looks left and right for the safest escape route as its webbed feet push off the surface.

We finished off the last bottle of wine over a week ago and have been drinking water ever since. But hidden in the bottom of the fridge, Joni saved four cans of soda. She fills our tumblers, adds a couple of small ice cubes, and hollers at us from the galley. "Come get your soda pops."

We lounge in the cockpit for over an hour, enjoying the scenery and basking in the fact that we have finally arrived, safe and in no hurry to get back in the race.

Ian gets up and bounces across the tramp into the cockpit. "Now that we're all qualified, who's gonna get an anchor tattoo?"

"Are we qualified because we sailed the Atlantic?" asks Joni.

"Definitely, and more," says Ian. "If you have sailed five thousand miles, you can wear a swallow tattoo. Over ten thousand miles, you're qualified for two swallows."

Tattooing has been a sailing tradition for hundreds of years. Reportedly, it became popular with Captain Cook's crew members during the voyages of exploration in the Pacific when the seafarers picked it up from the Polynesians.

With my right hand, I tap the outside of my left arm just below the shoulder. "If I ever get a tattoo, it'll be a black anchor right here."

Ian finishes the rest of his soda and adds, "And, if we sail around the treacherous Cape Horn, we'll be entitled to a fully rigged ship tattoo."

"Not doin' that one," says Ted. "But we'll be qualified for the five-thousand mile swallow when *Toucan* sails into Florida Bay."

"What about you, Joni?" I ask. "Would you get a tattoo?"

"No tattoos for me, but I'm about ready to get my feet back on solid ground and find a cold margarita to swallow."

"Yes, *terra firma* here we come." I extend my right hand shaped like I'm holding a beer. "And a chilled brewski for me."

Several times during the crossing I pondered another question—whether I'd ever sail across the ocean again. Now, reclining in the beauty of a safe harbor, I can't see myself making another passage. I'll be coastal cruising and island hopping from now on.

Does Ian feel the same way? "Hey Ian, how would you compare this trip to your previous crossing?"

"No comparison, this trip was perfect. Good friends, great chow, super boat, excellent weather."

"Excellent weather? Oh, that's right. You missed the storms on the way to the Canaries. Would you sail across Mother Ocean again?"

"Don't think so," says Ian. "First of all, my wife would disown me. And secondly, now I'm spoiled. How could any future crossing be better?" He smiles at Ted and Joni.

What a nice thing to say. I pause to let the weight of his compliment sink in. "What about you, skipper?"

"Definitely not," says Ted. "We're staying close to shore from now on. I said it before, and I'll say it again. I can't tell you how many times I worried about one of us getting sick or hurt."

Joni raises her tumbler. "Poseidon, the protector of seafarers, was watching out for us."

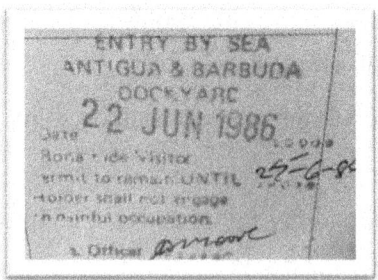

Ted eventually works his way out of the red bean bag and stretches. "Get your passports ready. Ian and I will go in first and get 'em stamped."

Ever since departing Santa Cruz, our inflatable Avon raft has been tied to the tramp but now it floats off the stern ready to carry us ashore. Ian climbs in with the oars and mutters, "There must be a brew pub or canteen nearby."

Ted taps his wristwatch and says, "I'll set my watch to local time and be back as soon as I can." He carries four passports protected in a Ziploc bag and carefully lowers himself into the raft. At Nelson's Dockyard, Ian hops out and ties up the dinghy eager to satisfy his thirst.

After Ted checks in with the Customs and Immigration office, he rows back out here to get me and Joni. Climbing aboard, he says, "They gave us bona fide three-day visitor's permits without any hassles."

The visa stamps read "Entry by Sea."

***

On Nelson's patio, we find Ian sitting in a rattan chair at a table for four. He looks quite relaxed with one of those mini parasols sticking through the top buttonhole of his shirt, the rum punch in his hand half empty. A frangipani tree behind him reaches for light over a hedge of croton.

Joni says, "Hey sailor, mind if we join you?"

He uncrosses his legs and sits up straight. "I would be so delighted." Which reminds me of that line in Zappa's "Sharleena."

Ted pulls a chair out for Joni while I take the seat next to Ian. "You've got the right idea."

When the waiter returns, Ted orders a margarita for Joni and a Manhattan on the rocks with a dash of bitters for himself.

The waiter looks my way. "And a bottle of Red Stripe for me."

Ian finishes his second rum punch. "I need to call my wife. I'll be back shortly."

Colorful, tame bullfinches perch on the backs of empty chairs, and one jumps on the brim of the sugar bowl. We watch Joni while she tries to get it to land on her finger. But soon the waiter arrives and like always, he chases the birds away. Joni gives him an evil eye.

Nearby, outside the customs office in one of those red phone booths, Ian holds the door open with his foot while he waits for the operator to get his wife to accept an overseas collect call. When he returns to the table, Joni takes another sip of her margarita with salt on the rim. "So, what'd she say?"

"She was glad to hear we made it okay but was not pleased to hear that I'll be gone for another two or three weeks."

Joni says, "She'll get over it."

"I hope so." Ian sounds like a worried man. "Keep your fingers crossed."

***

After lunch we visit the chandlery and Ted asks about replacement parts for the autohelm. The salesclerk says, "We can place an order for you, but delivery will take at least two weeks."

"Damn. We can't stay that long. Thanks anyway." Ted starts to leave when Joni nudges him. "Oh, there's one other thing. Does Duncan still work here?"

"That's me. Been here forever, but my last name's not Nelson." He's joking with us as he refers to Horatio Nelson, the famous British Admiral from the 1780s for whom the dockyard was named.

"We heard you could recommend a good restaurant."

"Sure can." He opens a drawer under the counter and pulls out a stack of business cards. "For dinner you might want to go into town."

Shuffling through the stack, he finds the one he's looking for and hands it to Ted. "All the taxi drivers in town know about Ms. Lizzy's place. You won't be disappointed."

Ted heads for the door. "Thanks a bunch."

Instead of taking taxicabs for the next couple of days, he rents a four-door sedan to venture into St. John's, the capital city. By the time we arrive, most of the tourists have returned to their cruise ships for the evening. We find Lizzy's near Redcliffe Quay and treat Joni to some fine dining on the terrace, fresh Caribbean Creole cuisine.

During a lull in the conversation, I offer my regrets. "You know I'd love to sail up to Florida with you, but I have to get back to work. I'm already a week overdue."

"You could retire about twenty years early," says Ted with a smile. "But we understand. It'll take us another two weeks to get back to St. Pete and you wouldn't have a job left by then."

"Probably not, but I feel like I'm leaving the party too early."

***

After dinner when we're back on *Toucan* with some liquid refreshments, I check the satnav one final time. The catamaran has been at anchor all afternoon, and the last two readings are only a second off. When I tell Ted about it, he says, "Now that the boat is stable, I'll take a quick sighting with the sextant to check its accuracy."

He removes the instrument from its box on the bench and starts turning knobs. I take another swig of Red Stripe. "Didn't you already align the mirrors?"

Ted holds the sextant with one hand like an expert and splashes another shot of bourbon on the lonely ice cubes in his tumbler. "The sextant is fine. I want to see if the satnav readings are correct."

Sitting at the table, Ian and I both crack a smile. Another beautiful night in paradise showers us with plenty of fixed stars even with the light of the full Moon.

"Good night." Joni finishes her wine. "I'll let you guys have fun with your toys."

Ted goes forward by the tramp to take a sighting on Polaris. I hand Ian the slip of paper with the coordinates from the satnav. "We'll see if he can match the latitude."

It's not long before Ted gets his sight and joins us at the table. He retrieves his tumbler, opens his notebook and says, "Here's my reading."

Ian makes a comparison. "You aren't gonna believe this. The numbers are close, within about ten seconds of latitude."

Ted looks out toward the Atlantic. "If I take another sighting with this tipsy sextant, it could put us out in the channel south of the island."

Gesturing toward the cabin, "I'll check the satnav later, and we'll still be right here, unless of course, the wind swings us on the anchor."

We finish our drinks, and Ted hits the sack. Ian helps tidy up the cockpit and glances my way. "It's been a fun trip."

"Couldn't have been much better." I reach out and shake his hand. "When you get to St. Pete, we could sail on my boat down the coast to

Key West for a couple of days." I step away then continue. "On the way back, drop anchor in the Dry Tortugas for a night. Wheel and deal with the guys on the fishing boats and maybe get a Spanish mackerel in trade for a six pack."

Ian looks thoughtful. "Sounds great, but my wife would go bonkers."

"Make it some other time. It's an open invitation."

We both hit the bunks, anticipating a quiet, uninterrupted good night's rest—like for more than four hours.

In the morning, Ian stays with the boat while Ted and Joni take me to the airport on the north side of the island. At the departure gate, Ted hands me a paperback. "I finished Campbell's book, the one you were browsing through last week. You might find it interesting."

"Thanks, I'll check it out." I slip the book in my shoulder bag and regard my friend with a smile. "It's been four weeks we'll never forget. Give me a call when you get home, and I'll come over to continue celebrating."

Joni has her sunglasses in her hand. "Yeah, and we'll watch the movie Ted made during the storm with Shuttleworth at the helm."

With another big smile I say, "We'll have to show it to him someday."

Out on the taxiway a truck with a metal staircase fastened on top pulls up and parks by the forward door of the plane. The ticket taker at the gate motions for the passengers to begin boarding. I really don't want to leave. Joni gives me a quick hug and I shake Ted's hand.

At the top of the steps before entering the aircraft, I turn around to wave but at the last second touch my forehead with a salute.

 # Epilogue

I arrived back in St. Pete still feeling queasy about my decision to leave Ted and Joni in Antigua. On that first night home, I grabbed a folding lawn chair off the front porch and walked around the corner to Lake Sheffield, a neighborhood pond surrounded by palm trees. The waning Moon rose, and its light rippled on the water. I closed my eyes, knowing that *Toucan* was catching the same glow. A tear welled up as I pictured them at the table under the boom, then I chuckled remembering Ian's flying fish and his pseudo dinner jacket.

They soon cruised northwest from Antigua through the Virgin Islands, skirted along the north shores of Puerto Rico, past Hispaniola, up through Channel Five in the Florida Keys, then home to Tierra Verde.

I still wish I had been along for the last part of the trip.

In the years following, I often looked back with fond memories of fulfilling my dream and treasured the sixteen days spent crossing the Atlantic. That peaceful time with compatible friends sharing responsibilities, cooperating in all ways, day after day, rewarded me with a different view of life, of humanity, of the planet.

If you ask me, I'd encourage anyone to consider taking a long trip into the wilderness. Step away for a while from the daily routine, from phones, TVs, and computers. Learn to appreciate, fall in love with, and cherish Mother Earth, the only *Pale Blue Dot*.

 ## About the Author

Doug Fricke has sailed on a wide variety of boats, both as crew and as skipper. He learned in the mid-1970s with his Hobie Cat off the beaches of Florida. In the early '80s he upgraded to a Stiletto catamaran and by the mid-80s became the second owner of a 38' Newick Native trimaran custom-built by Concordia Yachts.

Along the way, he obtained a U.S. Coast Guard captain's license for chartering, organized regattas in Tampa Bay, acted as committee chairman for the Stiletto Nationals in Sarasota, and later worked as a part-time instructor with the Offshore Sailing School in Jersey City.

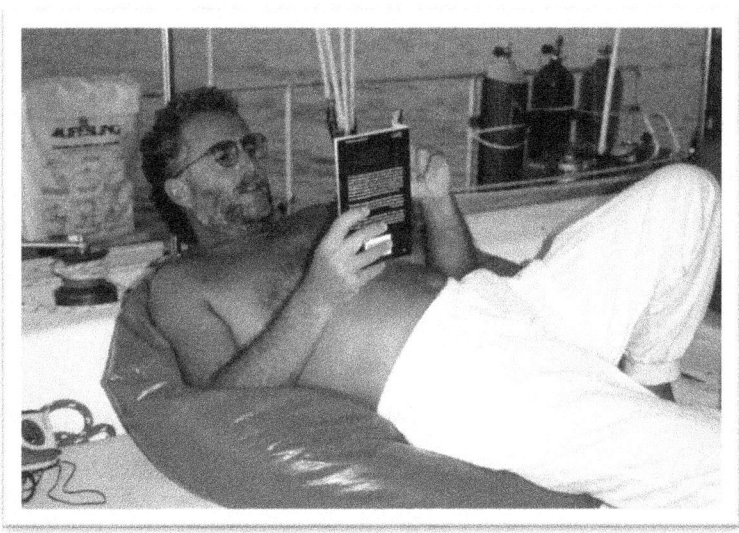

The author onboard *Toucan* in the Florida Keys in April 1994, eight years after the Atlantic crossing.

 # Acknowledgements

When my wife wasn't reading a mystery novel, knitting, or tending to the cats and plants, she would listen as I recalled the details of the same old sailing story. Without her patience and encouragement, this novella would not have been published. Thanks Judy.

Special thanks to Rich Wells, Stephan Loy, Linda Sammaritan, the Wilber Team, Sasha Virjee, Joy Tobin, Dean Howell, and other members of the Indianapolis Writers Group for their numerous critiques.

Champion sailor Mike Speth, friend and first place competitor at the Stiletto Nationals, reviewed an early edition for best sailing and boat handling techniques.

Mr. Dave Jones, a retired instructor at the US Power Squadron in Natick, Massachusetts, reviewed the chapter on celestial navigation.

Thanks to beta readers Sheila Streeter and Joany DeVries for their constructive criticism and honest feedback.

On separate occasions, professional editors Erica Converso and Matt McAvoy provided excellent guidance for correcting and improving the manuscript.

Finally, thanks to boat designer extraordinaire and friend John Shuttleworth for permission to use his name.

1st Place in Non-fiction, Travel / Adventure category

"Throughout the voyage, they face terrible storms and damage to their vessel. However, the team learns to appreciate their amazing surroundings, nature, and many different cultures."

Lesley Jones for Readers' Favorite

2023 Independent Author Network "Book of the Year" Award for Non-fiction in the Travel / Nature category

"Wrapped inside this straightforward and compelling story, Mr. Fricke seamlessly ties in some very important messages about our relationship to nature."

Joseph W. Hudgens, Author of "Saturn: The Cassini Division"

www.ingramcontent.com/pod-product-compliance
Lightning Source LLC
Chambersburg PA
CBHW060321050426
42449CB00011B/2593